The
False
Prophet

The
False
Prophet

DWIGHT E. STEVENSON

New York ABINGDON PRESS Nashville

THE FALSE PROPHET

Copyright © 1965 by Abingdon Press

Library of Congress Catalog Card Number: 65-13058

Scripture quotations unless otherwise noted are from the
Revised Standard Version of the Bible, copyrighted 1946
and 1952 by the Division of Christian Education, National
Council of Churches, and are used by permission.

Scripture passages noted NEB are from *The New English
Bible, New Testament.* © The Delegates of the Oxford
University Press and the Syndics of the Cambridge
University Press 1961. Reprinted by permission.

SET UP, PRINTED, AND BOUND BY THE
PARTHENON PRESS, AT NASHVILLE,
TENNESSEE, UNITED STATES OF AMERICA

Dedicated to the memory of
Marion Stevenson
(1861-1945)
known as "Dad" to thousands;
as my uncle, to me he was
a second father
faithful to God
true to himself
false to no man

Preface

Michelangelo once explained to an inquirer how he turned a block of marble into a sculptured masterpiece. He said something like this: "The statue is there in the marble, waiting to be released. All I do is to knock off the excess stone."

The uncovering of the true prophet in each Christian minister is not unlike this. At the beginning, every preacher is, at best, a prophet in the rough. The authentic messenger of God lies within, waiting to be released. In the meantime he is hidden or obscured by inauthentic elements which must be chiseled off or polished away. Knock off the false, and the truth stands revealed; eliminate the fraudulent, and the genuine appears.

The making of a preacher is not quite that simple. There is much positive work to be done, but as a teacher of preaching for many years, I have learned the power of negative examples. Let a man catch another doing something wrong and let him identify the mistake as one not unlike his own. Lead him to analyze it and find his way thereby to positive principles. The chances are very good that he will have a never-to-be-forgotten lesson.

I have long thought that we could learn a great deal about our prophetic mission by looking more closely at the biblical figure of the false prophet. We are living through a time when both church and ministry are seeking renewal. No small part of that renewal lies in the recovery of a clear sense of mission. Or, to put the matter in terms of current jargon, there is a search for a clear "image" of the ministry. This book seeks to contribute to a sharper image of the Christian ministry by sounding a warning against the false and the counterfeit, especially as it applies to the pulpit ministry and as it lies revealed in the biblical indictment of false prophecy.

False prophecy arises from a distortion within institutionalized religion. Specifically, it arises from the demonic. It may well be that the key heresy of our age is not disbelief in God but disbelief in the demonic. While he was one of the editors of *Time,* Whittaker Chambers wrote an article entitled "The Devil," which appeared in the February 2, 1948, issue of *Life* magazine. The article discussed the proposition that Satan, having gone underground, is now carrying out the most subtle and successful temptation of his long, blackhearted career: He is convincing millions of good people that he no longer exists! While not subscribing to the belief in a personal devil, this book does take Satan seriously; and it finds the church to be one of Satan's favorite spheres of operation, his undercover agent being the false prophet.

The war between God and Satan is waged, not merely between the church and the world, but also and even centrally

8

within the religious institution itself. The church will arrive at its own function and achieve its proper glory only as it recognizes and fights against the temptations of the unreal and the inauthentic in its own life. And the ministry, by the same measure, will be fulfilled only by men who fight against the tendency toward fraudulence in themselves. This is one of the reasons why the Protestant reformers insisted that the church of the Reformation must always be a reforming church—reforming itself as the essential condition to any work of reformation that it may be able to do in the world. A church—a ministry—seeking renewal cannot avoid encountering the false prophet who lives within its own precincts. Only through such an encounter and the consequent battle may the church recover the voice of true proclamation.

Let the reader be warned against a premature identification of the false prophet. And let him not suppose that this book advocates a new witch hunt. If he reads the book to the end, he may find himself asking—like the disciples in the Upper Room on the eve of the Crucifixion—"Lord, is it I?"

The chapters of this book, except the final one, were first delivered as lectures in the twelfth annual Spring Lectureship at The College of the Bible (Lexington Theological Seminary) where, since 1947, it has been my privilege to teach preaching. Five of the lectures were subsequently repeated at Union Theological Seminary of Virginia. The gracious reception accorded the lectures on both occasions encouraged me to write a concluding chapter and to offer the manuscript for publication in book form. Here let me express to President-Emeritus Riley B. Montgomery and to my own colleagues on the faculty in Lexington, Kentucky, my deep thanks for being invited to this lectureship in 1964. My thanks also to the students and friends of the seminary who heard me out with such encouraging courtesy. I should like, further, to extend my gratitude to President James A. Jones and Robert W. Kirkpatrick of Union Theological Seminary of Virginia, who brought me before a stimulating audience of ministers from many parts of the United States and Canada. Thanks are due also to Miss Marilyn Williams, one of the faculty secretaries, who typed the manuscript.

DWIGHT E. STEVENSON

Contents

Contents

The Enemy
Within
the Gate

One of the most interesting—and most sinister—figures to appear within the story of the Bible is the false prophet. He moves across the pages of both Testaments. Sometimes he is a skulking figure darting through shadows of back alleys. More often he is comfortably lodged in palace or temple, a well-known and fully accepted member of the religious establishment, dressed in fine robes and faring sumptuously. He is detected with difficulty, if at all; and exposed infrequently.

THE FALSE PROPHET—A FAMILIAR FIGURE

When Jehoshaphat and Ahab joined forces to recapture Ramoth-gilead from Syria in the middle of the ninth century B.C., Ahab called upon a whole troop of accredited prophets who supported the venture. The lone prophet Micaiah called their prophecy false—and landed in prison on a bread and water diet for his pains. The duel between true and false prophets thus initiated continued with little letup to the end of the biblical record. No one fought this duel with greater vigor than Jeremiah. (See Jer. 23:9-40 in particular.) Outnumbered, frequently outmaneuvered, Jeremiah nevertheless thrust and parried with all his strength. Perhaps no one in antiquity did more to alert Israel to the danger within its own ranks.

> An appalling and horrible thing
>   has happened in the land:
> the prophets prophesy falsely,
>   and the priests rule at their direction;
> my people love to have it so (Jer. 5:30-31).

Thus Jeremiah states both the prevalence and the perniciousness of the danger.

The Deuteronomic law provided the full severity of the death penalty for anyone convicted of prophesying falsely (Deut. 13:5). But, as a careful reading of the Old Testament will show, more often it was the true prophet who was discredited, arrested, imprisoned, and executed. Without honor in his own time and in his own country, he came into his own only in later centuries.

The irony of this reversal did not escape Jesus; therefore he addressed his contemporaries as the spiritual "sons of those who murdered the prophets" (Matt. 23:31). The distinction between a true and false prophet is easy to detect only in retrospect, and may not be absolutely certain even then. Jesus challenges as delusion our easy assumption that we would have known better if we had been there. We say, "If we had lived in the days of our fathers, we would not have taken part with them in shedding the blood of the prophets" (Matt. 23:30). But in actual fact we have more to do with adorning tombs and building monuments to prophets of the past than with listening to those of our own generation. We find it easier to listen to the false prophets while honoring false prophets as true and branding true prophets false. It is this fact, so well documented in the biblical record and so well attested to in our own social history, that makes the threat of the false prophet so insidious.

It may come as a surprise that the false prophet receives even more attention in the New Testament than he does in the Old. Jesus spoke against them: "Beware of false prophets, who come to you in sheep's clothing but inwardly are ravenous wolves" (Matt. 7:15). Paul and Barnabas encountered and dealt with one such prophet on the island of Cyprus (Acts 13:4-12). Paul denounced sham apostles in Corinth and in Galatia (II Cor. 11:3; Gal. 1:6-7). The Johannine writings warn against them: "Beloved, do not believe every spirit, but test the spirits to see whether they are of God; for many false prophets have gone out into the world" (I John 4:1). The late Second Letter of Peter is no less cautionary: "But false prophets also arose among the people, just as there will be false teachers among you, who will secretly bring in destructive heresies, even denying the Master who bought them, bringing upon themselves swift destruction" (II Peter 2:1). Within the biblical story, the false prophet does not meet his fate until the judgment, when in flaming apocalypse he is unmasked and his work of deception is ended (Rev. 16:13; 19:20).

From this quick sampling of Old Testament and New it becomes clear that the false prophet is a prominent figure upon the biblical landscape and that biblical religion takes him quite seriously as an enemy within the gates. It is further obvious that false prophecy does not succeed unless it deceives. The false prophet comes forth disguised as a knight in the armor of truth. At this point an interesting question arises: He deceives; is he also self-deceived?

DECEIVER AND SELF-DECEIVED

Professional religion now has and has always had its share of "quacks." Wolves in sheep's clothing who know that they are wolves have from the beginning infiltrated the flock. But it is easier to deceive some flocks than others, and these for the most part are flocks of young sheep. That is to say, impostors are drawn especially to new religious movements. These racketeers sense in the new and unstructured life of a young movement a larger scope of freedom for their predatory operations. This fact recently came home to me with new force as I was reading about Alexander Campbell and the Disciples of Christ in the 1830's. On more than one occasion Campbell found it necessary to warn the readers of the *Millennial Harbinger* against itinerating "impostors." In October, 1837, he published a letter of warning from Lewis County, Kentucky:

A few weeks ago a young man of light complexion, light hair, somewhat inclined to curl, five feet and eight inches high, and calling himself *Henry C. Gilbert,* made his appearance in Lewis County, under the mask of a preacher of the Ancient Gospel. To some of the less informed brethren he produced a letter, which could not be read in consequence of the badness of the writing; but when more inquisitive and better informed brethren desired to see it, he at first pretended he had lost it, then positively declined showing it, and finally left them just before the time appointed by himself for a two days' meeting; and has been heard of since making his way up the Ohio canal.[1]

In the December issue of the same magazine, Campbell published another warning over his own initials:

Brother Shepard, of the "Primitive Christian," New York, has published *J. H. Lamphear,* now in Portage county, Ohio, as a polygamist and unworthy of the name of a Christian. He is from all accounts, certainly unworthy the confidence of the Christian communion as a *teacher* of religion. I trust I shall not be sued for this notice, as in the case of W. W. Sleigh. Impostors must be exposed and Christians protected from wolves in the garb of sheep, at all risks and perils.[2]

To clear up the reference to being sued by W. W. Sleigh, let me say that several years before Alexander Campbell had accused W. W. Sleigh, a traveling religious lecturer, of swindling and embezzlement, whereupon Sleigh sued Campbell for $10,000 "damages to his fair name and saintly reputation." The trial commenced in the Supreme Court of Pennsylvania, but was settled by arbitration requiring no less than thirty meetings over a period of about four years. It was not settled until August 4, 1838, when Campbell was successful in making his charges stick.[3]

Incidents like these from the early history of an American religious movement make it easier to understand the cautions sounded in the second century by the *Didache:*

About apostles and prophets, follow the rule of the Gospel, which is this: Let every apostle who comes to you be welcomed as the

---

[1] *Millennial Harbinger* (October, 1837), p. 480.
[2] *Ibid.* (December, 1837), p. 574.
[3] *Ibid.* (February, 1836), pp. 91, 548; (October, 1938), pp. 462-65, 478.

Lord. But he shall not stay more than one day, and if it is necessary, the next day also. But if he stays three days, he is a false prophet. And when an apostle leaves, let him take nothing except bread to last until he finds his next lodging. But if he asks for money, he is a false prophet.[4]

The church has always had a few predators. Sinclair Lewis could have written *Elmer Gantry* in almost any century since Pentecost. But the out-and-out impostor, the deceiver who is not self-deceived, is rare; and he is not a serious threat. Sooner or later he will be recognized and punished.

For the most part, the impression that we get from the Bible is that the false prophets were men of great earnestness and sincerity. They deceived others, to be sure; but before that they were self-deceived. In their own eyes they were false neither to man nor God.

It is interesting to notice that Micaiah, in opposing the prophets who supported Ahab's campaign against Syria, did not accuse them of insincerity. Instead, he said, they were duped, duped by God himself in order to bring upon Ahab the judgment that was his due:

And Micaiah said, "Therefore hear the word of the Lord: I saw the Lord sitting on his throne, and all the host of heaven standing beside him on his right hand and on his left; and the Lord said, 'Who will entice Ahab, that he may go up and fall at Ramoth-gilead?' And one said one thing, and another said another. Then a spirit came forward and stood before the Lord, saying, 'I will entice him.' And the Lord said to him, 'By what means?' And he said, 'I will go forth, and will be a lying spirit in the mouth of all his prophets.' And he said, 'You are to entice him, and you shall succeed; go forth and do so'" (I Kings 22:19-22).

[4] The *Didache* vi: 3-6, *The Apostolic Fathers, an American Translation*, trans. Edgar J. Goodspeed (New York: Harper & Brothers, 1950), p. 16.

No sooner had Micaiah given his somewhat ingenious explanation than Zedekiah, one of the accused prophets, strode up to him and in righteous indignation struck him in the face. And he said, "How did the Spirit of the Lord go from me to speak to you?" That is to say, Zedekiah was clear in his own mind that he had spoken the very word of God, and that Micaiah, not he, was the liar. An examination of false prophets through the rest of the Bible shows them in much the same light. These men often had a fanatical certainty of their own correctness. They had zeal. They were sincere. And they were sure that the true prophets who opposed them—from Amos through Jeremiah and from Jesus through Paul—were agents of Beelzebub.

It is at this point that we have come upon the depth and complexity of the problem of the false prophet. He is a destroyer of true religion, but he thinks of himself as its protector. He sees as enemy the one whom God has marked as friend. Within the life of the church this throws us into a contradiction having no obvious solution. Two equally earnest men in equal sincerity stand facing each other. Each thinks he is right and that the other is wrong. Each accuses the other of false prophecy.

This has several logical inferences: If sincerity of belief is no guarantee of authenticity, we shall have to find other standards of truth, other guarantees. But what are these? If the false prophet does not know that he is false, we are faced with the possibility that any one of us, or all of us together, may actually be enrolled among the false prophets. We, who pride ourselves on being Christian soldiers, may actually be fighting against God. And we are not free to dismiss this shocking possibility lightly. Finally, the presence of the self-

19

deceived false prophet in the bosom of the church presents us with the church's greatest danger. The ultimate peril to the church does not arise in attack from without. It lies in subversion—albeit unconscious subversion—undermining from within. It lies in a kind of piety which is really blasphemy; in a kind of loyalty which is really treason; in a kind of religion which is really atheism.

THE INSIDEDNESS OF THE PERIL

It is the last inference that we must now examine. We may call it the "insidedness" of the church's peril—the enemy within the gates. It is deeper than any conscious apostasy, more insidious than outright secularism, more virulent than conspiracy.

To see the problem with any depth, we must turn to the idea of the demonic. The Apostle Paul made the connection between false prophesy and the demonic quite explicit in his harsh letter to the Corinthians. The section is worth reading as a whole:

And what I do I will continue to do, in order to undermine the claim of those who would like to claim that in their boasted mission they work on the same terms as we do. For such men are false apostles, deceitful workmen, disguising themselves as apostles of Christ. And no wonder, for even Satan disguises himself as an angel of light. So it is not strange if his servants also disguise themselves as servants of righteousness (II Cor. 11:12-15).

There are three ideas in this passage relevant to our investigation: (1) The reality of the demonic. (2) The masquerade of the demonic under the forms of righteousness.

20

(3) The identification of false prophets as servants of the demonic.

Look first at the reality of the demonic. Under the spell of "factualism," modern man has tried to dismiss the figure of Satan as though he were nothing more than a species of delirium tremens. If we have ushered God to the borders of his universe, allowing him to exist but not at the center, we have been even more ruthless with Satan. We have banished him altogether. When the orthodoxy of this age is finally assessed by a future generation of theologians, it may be found that our worst heresy is not refusal to believe in God but our refusal to believe in Satan. For by making Satan unreal we make the struggle against him unreal, and reduce God to an indulgent Grandfather in heaven.

Do not misunderstand me. I am not arguing for belief in a personal devil. I am not at all sure that evil is a single entity, let alone intentional. I doubt if the evil forces of this world could get together to form a committee, let alone elect a dictator. But this is not to say that evil is neither real nor superhuman, or that it lacks the power to cast us into hell.

We can lay the ontological question to one side. It is not necessary to discover the ultimate status of evil in or before the Godhead. We cannot help speculation about that, perhaps, but evil as we confront it in human life is not a metaphysical abstraction. It is exactly what the name *Satan* denotes—the adversary. For evil as we experience it is not mere absence of good. It is not simply "cultural lag." It is a nihilistic force, a destructive power working within and among us—within us but against us.

In locating these nihilistic forces we do not agree with our biblical ancestors. For, whereas they tended to locate the headquarters of the demons in outer space, we find their locus in the human unconscious and in certain folkways and institutions. That is to say, our ancestors thought of demonology as a branch of astrology, whereas we think of it as a branch of depth psychology and sociology.

Our biblical ancestors put it like this: "For we are not contending against flesh and blood, but against the principalities, against the powers, against the world rulers of this present darkness, against the spiritual hosts of wickedness in the heavenly places" (Eph. 6:12).

Today we would not put this in the form of demonology and astrology. We would state it in terms of neuroses, compulsions, and obsessions that lurk deep in the black caverns of the mind. We would further locate it in the inherited injustices of society which put some men in chains and hold others under oppression through the sheer accident of birth or of skin color. We would locate it in social habits like war and crime; in structures of tyrannical power, in diabolical propaganda, in greed and lust, in the passionate hatreds that made words of reproach of such names as Dachau, Auschwitz, and Buchenwald. These enemies are worse than communism, because they maintain a recruiting station inside us. The scripture is quite realistic when it says that we fight not against human foes, but "against cosmic powers . . . against superhuman forces." That is how the New English Bible translates it. Who will say that this scripture is not talking about reality as we have known it? What does it matter if the New Testament located these evils in the heights of upper air and we locate them, under different names, in the depths of the unconscious?

Several months ago Harry Asher, an English psysiologist,

submitted to a clinical experiment in which he was administered one thirty millionths of a gram of *lysergic acid diethylamide,* more popularly known as LSD. He reported the experiment in an article entitled, "They Split My Personality." Let me quote a few paragraphs from this report:

There were two of me walking down the corridor. The two people were not very accurately localized in space, but the main one corresponded in position to where I would have been had there been only one of me. The shadowy, or more tenuous individual, the naughty one, was slightly to the left. We could talk to each other, exchanging verbal thoughts, but not talking aloud.

The main person was really me, but in an improved form. He was a very strong character. He had an effortless strength that I never knew before that I possessed. The other individual on the left was much less well known to me. "Why not jump out of a window?" he said to me.

He was driven home from the office by an assistant. But when he found himself at the door of his house he declined to go in. " 'No, thank you, darling, I think I won't come in just now,' I said to my wife. 'I will go for a walk. Keep the children away from me, will you please?' "

Then he explains to the reader: "I had a compulsive urge to do violence to my children, and did not like to tell her about it." [5]

Episode after episode piles up to show the "shadowy self" within the self as a completely selfish, completely loveless, and ruthless character who wanted to destroy him and his own children and completely disarm him of willpower. Thus, through the use of drugs, one man unmasked within himself

---

[5] Harry Asher, "They Split My Personality," *Saturday Review* (June 1, 1963), pp. 41, 42.

the lower self who ordinarily speaks to us only after he has disguised himself in pleasing rationalizations. Man has known from antiquity that something like this was true. And now modern science is beginning to validate it. The "shadowy selves" struggle up from the dark abyss of our own beings, seeking to gain mastery over us and to carry out their death wish. It would be harder to find a more illuminating commentary upon the observation of First John: "He who does not love remains in death" (I John 3:14). This selfishness is a primeval force within us, an antagonist with demonic vitality. In describing the threat to our life which rises out of this abyss we need dark, apocalyptic words, like those of Martin Luther's *Ein Feste Burg;*

> For still our ancient foe
> Doth seek to work us woe;
> His craft and power are great,
> And, armed with cruel hate,
> On earth is not his equal.

After this comment on the reality of the demonic, there is little that we need to say about the masquerade of the demonic under the forms of righteousness. Paul said that false apostles disguise themselves as apostles of Christ: "And no wonder, for even Satan diguises himself as an angel of light." Ever since Sigmund Freud exposed the "censor" and laid bare the escape mechanisms of projection and rationalization, we have had the modern means of understanding this. And, indeed, the human race has always known this dark secret about its hidden motivations. Jeremiah knew it more than six centuries before Christ: "The heart is deceitful above all things, and desperately corrupt; who can understand it?" (Jer. 17:9).

But, see what this means in the life of religious institutions and in the personal religious life. It means that the house of God is also the synagogue of Satan. It means that much religion—even sincere and zealous religion—is false.

EVIL IN RELIGION

Thus, once again, we need to stand corrected by biblical understanding. We have been inclined to think of all religion as good and to look with approval upon all faiths. Our taxis on Saturday afternoon and evening carry the sign: "Attend the church of your choice." We are a churchgoing nation, a nation of people caught in religious pluralism who nevertheless are greatly in favor of religion in general. So true is this that Peter Berger and Martin E. Marty say that we have in America an extralegal religious establishment, just as much as, perhaps even more than, any country with a state church. Religion, any religion, we regard as good; atheism, any atheism, we regard as bad. The Bible knows nothing of such a division between religion and irreligion. It only knows about the worship of the one true God as opposed to the worship of idols. It only knows about good religion *versus* bad religion; true faith *versus* bad faith. And it knows further that whereas the way of true faith is narrow, steep, and difficult—a road of hardest resistance—the way of bad faith is a road of least resistance. One falls into it without trying. This is simply to say that it is easier to worship Baal, a false god, than it is to worship the God and Father of our Lord Jesus Christ. It is easier to worship Satan than God, even in the house of God.

One has but to recall the long, sorry story of man's inhumanity to man in the name of high religion. Consider, for example, the recapture of Jerusalem by Christian knights in A.D. 1099. Centuries earlier the Moslem Caliph Omar (in A.D. 638) had entered Jerusalem in pilgrim robe, on foot, without bloodshed, but kneeling in prayer in the outer courts of the Church of the Holy Sepulcher. When the Christian knights came, the story was far different: On June 7, 1099 Bohemund and Godfrey with twelve thousand knights stood before the walls of Jerusalem. The Fatimid caliph then in control of the Holy City offered to make peace, pledging safety to Christian pilgrims and worshipers in Jerusalem. The Crusaders refused the offer, demanding unconditional surrender instead. A siege of forty days following in which the Fatimid garrison of one thousand men resisted twelve thousand knights. On July 15, the city was captured. According to Raymond of Agiles, an eyewitness: "Numbers of the Saracens were beheaded . . . others were shot with arrows, or forced to jump from the towers; others were tortured for several days and then burned in flames. In the streets were seen piles of heads and hands and feet. One rode about everywhere amid the corpses of men and horses."

Will Durant, who cites the above description, goes on to supply other details from his research into the event. "Women were stabbed . . . suckling babes were snatched by the leg from their mothers' breasts and . . . their necks broken . . . against posts." The seventy thousand Moslems living in the Holy City were massacred. All the Jews were herded into a synagogue and burned alive. Thereafter, according to Durant, "The victors flocked to the church of the Holy Sepulcher, whose grotto, they believed, had once held the crucified Christ.

There, embracing one another, they wept with joy and release, and thanked the God of Mercies for their victory." [6]

One can think, too, of the inhumanity of man to man in the name of Christian orthodoxy: The promoters of the Spanish Inquisition breaking men on the rack, tearing out their tongues —all in the name of holy faith. The people of Florence burning Savonarola at the stake. The city of Geneva, with Calvin's blessing, martyring Servetus. Luther's wars on the Anabaptists.

Or come nearer to our own time. Ministers of the gospel of Christ believing and preaching that the Negro had no soul, that the institution of slavery merely carried out God's curse on Ham and that, therefore, it was a divinely ordained institution. And in our own day, fascism as virulent as the Nazi virus of the 1930's lives in America under religious slogans with ministers of religion as their protagonists.

No wonder Helvetius said: "What does the history of religions teach us? That religions have kindled the torch of intolerance everywhere. They have filled the plains with corpses, bathed the countryside in blood, destroyed cities, devastated empires." [7]

No wonder atheists with an acute social conscience, from Karl Marx to H. L. Mencken, have branded all religion false and have looked for the day when it would be extirpated from the human race like astrology and trial by ordeal. They have called for the abolition of religion in devotion to humanity and social justice.

This criticism of false religion coming from outside the church should arise from within. The prophetic voice of true

[6] Will Durant, *The Age of Faith* (New York: Simon and Schuster, 1950), p. 592.

[7] Reinhold Niebuhr, *The Nature and Destiny of Man* (New York: Charles Scribner's Sons, 1943), I, 97.

religion has always known that the abomination of desolation appears *in the temple.* And that voice has always warned that "judgment begins at the house of God."

Just as it is no service to God if we have buried the devil, it is no service to the church if we always praise it. It is not the church that is good; it is God who is good. The church is the realm of ultimate encounter, where we meet both God and his adversary. Or to say it more accurately, it is the realm of the human soul, as that soul becomes a battleground whereon God and Satan clash in the eschatological war—the eternal Armageddon.

False prophesy lives in the church; it thrives there; the church is its natural habitat. It arises from the abyss within us—the abyss of primeval selfishness, of our anxieties, our hatreds, or our death wish. And it erects its structures of self-righteousness. It builds its tower of religion to reach heaven and usurp the rule of God. This has led men like Karl Barth to say that Christianity is not a religion. The word *religion* scarcely appears in the Bible.[8] The New Testament has no sacerdotal apparatus to speak of. For biblical faith, with few exceptions, is not man reaching for God; it is God reaching for man.

At this point we are confronted by a double paradox. The adversary of man—the forces against us which we symbolize in the figure of Satan—does not appear as an adversary at all. He appears as an angel of light. He is urbane, he is a king of smiles, a benefactor bearing gifts. He promises the kingdoms of this world and the glory of them. Only when he is resisted

---

[8] See Acts 26:5; I Tim. 2:10; 3:16; II Tim. 3:5 and James 1:26-27, to which add Acts 17:22 and I Tim. 5:4 for the adjective *religious.* These references exhaust the Bible's use of the term.

does he reveal himself as our enemy. God, on the other hand, first appears as our enemy. From our position of moral rebellion we can only see him erroneously as the one who is against us. And he is against us, as a fireman is against fire breaking out of control and destroying a house. He is against us because he is for us. He wounds us as a surgeon wounds, in order to heal. He destroys as a building wrecker destroys to make room for a new and better building. Fundamentally he is creator, not destroyer. But he first appears as a destroyer, rooting up. We do not yet know that he is about to plant. He comes as a wrecker tearing down. We do not yet know that he will build.

This is where Satan and his prophets get their opportunity. They offer us security. Security—just another way of spelling death. Security—the return to the womb of the human mother or to the tomb of mother earth.

MAN-AT-BAY

Therefore, it comes about that much "religion" is man-at-bay before God, who demands of him that his heart be broken, that he die to his old self. In this extremity, man-at-bay bargains with the devil to pay his ransom so he can return to his old self-centered life without the inconvenience of a divine interruption or the pain of repentance.

As long as this is true there will be false prophets in the church. And we may be among them!

Captured
by Culture

Then Amaziah the priest of Bethel sent to Jeroboam king of
Israel, saying, "Amos has conspired against you in the midst of
the house of Israel; the land is not able to bear all his words.
For thus Amos has said,

> 'Jeroboam shall die by the sword,
> and Israel must go into exile
> away from his land.' "

And Amaziah said to Amos, "O seer, go, flee away to the land
of Judah, and eat bread there, and prophesy there; but never again
prophesy at Bethel, for it is the king's sanctuary and it is a temple
of the kingdom" (Amos 7:10-13).

In this incident from the book of Amos we have an almost
perfect instance of the clash of the true with the false prophet
in the realm of culture. It was, as both Amos and Hosea
showed, a culture sick unto death, a culture needing deep
surgery before there could be healing and without which there
could be no future. Amos called for that surgery, but Amaziah
mistook the instrument in the hand of Amos. It was a surgeon's

scalpel, but Amaziah thought it was an assassin's dagger. Amaziah was a priest of the living God by conscious intention, but in actual fact he was high priest of Israel's *status quo*. Thus, he did not say, "This is the sanctuary of God." He did say, "It is the king's sanctuary." He did not say, "It is a temple of the kingdom of God." He did say, "It is a temple of the kingdom" of Israel.

Captured by a culture that was even then entering its twilight hour, Amaziah thought himself to be the king's friend when in actual fact he was the king's enemy. He thought himself to be a loyal citizen, when all the time it was he who was the traitor. The false prophet always commits the mistake of making the king supreme and of trying to make God the king's servant. Or, to put it another way, the false prophet supposes that "our way of life" is the highest good, that it deserves to be eternal, and that the church exists to defend and preserve that way of life.

The false prophet is a citizen of his world, but not a free citizen. This is because he does not see deeply into his world, or, as Jesus said, he can read the signs of the weather but he cannot read the signs of the times.

Kyle Haselden, editor of *The Christian Century*, recently wrote,

Historically, the prophet is one who stands in an intimate relationship to the history of his own time, but his message is directed not to the superficial waves of his time but to the deep Gulf Streams which flow beneath the surface of life. He sees as others do not the dominant and decisive trends and the immediate and ultimate outcome of those trends. Historians can interpret historical events after they happen. Prophets understand the trends of the

31

times while they are happening. To study the prophets of old is not to explore the antiquities but to discover the eternities.[1]

The false prophet does not have this deepgoing perception. Strictly speaking, he is no *seer;* he does not see. Instead he is devoted to the surface of life—to its waves, not to its Gulf Streams. He is modern and up-to-date, so up-to-date that with the passage of only a little time he will be obsolete.

A REALISTIC WORD ABOUT CULTURE

Before proceeding further it is necessary to be clear and realistic about culture. What do we mean by the term? Perhaps we could do no better than to accept the description of the late H. Richard Niebuhr of Yale University: "Culture is the 'artificial, secondary environment' which man superimposes on the natural. It comprises language, habits, ideas, beliefs, customs, social organization, inherited artifacts, technical processes, and values." [2]

With such a definition, culture and civilization become interchangeable terms. And both are equivalent to what the writer of the Fourth Gospel and the First Letter of John called "the world." We speak English but not as it is spoken in England or Australia. We eat with a knife and a fork and not with chopsticks; we eat oysters but not caterpillars. We support representative government, not a king or a dictator. We believe that disease is caused by germs, not by devils. When entering a house, our men take off their hats, but not their

[1] Kyle Haselden, *The Urgency of Preaching* (New York: Harper & Row, 1963), p. 98.
[2] H. Richard Niebuhr, *Christ and Culture* (New York: Harper & Brothers, 1951), p. 32.

shoes. We surround ourselves with hospitals, schools, factories, and stores, as well as with automobiles, refrigerators, radios, vacuum cleaners, and airplanes. We try criminals before courts of law, not through ordeal by fire or combat. We do not believe in slavery.

The list could be extended to an exceedingly long recital. It is this complex of special habits, customs, taboos, tools, machines, institutions, language, ideas, and ideals that forms the cultural world in which we all live and move and have our being. As long as we are human beings we cannot escape from it or live outside of it. And most of us do not even think that we want to.

When we live within that familiar complex we feel "at home." Out of it we feel like strangers or foreigners. I well recall the nameless feeling that I had recently as my wife and I drove by automobile across more than a dozen European and Near Eastern countries. At every frontier I bought new road maps; and, thanks to these, I seldom lost my way. But I kept thinking, "To understand a country you need several maps, superimposed one upon the other." For as you drive through a beautiful landscape, as through Saint Gotthard's Pass in the Swiss Alps, or up the Moselle Valley in Germany, or in the Peloponnesus area of Greece or across the tableland of Turkey south of Ankara, you drive not only on solid earth under a blue sky but also through an invisible landscape. Even when you see no people, this landscape is in evidence: in the way the fields are laid out, in the language of the road signs, in the work animals and the way they are harnessed, in the architecture of peasant houses, in the ruins of deserted castles. You feel that you are living at once in the real, tangible world of things and objects and also in a fairyland. So it is with all people; we all live in the world of nature and in the world of culture—on earth and in fairyland.

No cultural fairyland, of course, is perfect. Each has not only its bright spirits but also its dark demons. But normally we even prefer demons of our own culture to those of any species of foreign devils.

In the spring of 1961, while touring in Egypt, I ran out of Egyptian currency and went to the National Bank of Egypt in Cairo to cash some traveler's checks. I found others before me bent on the same mission. Three people immediately in front of me were of dark skin; I judged them to be from India. On talking with them I discovered that they were indeed Indians, but they were not from India. They were from South Africa. I also learned that the Egyptians had not strewn their pathway with palm branches and flowers during their eight-day visit to the land of the Nile; instead it had been a pathway strewn with thorns. To put it bluntly, they were disenchanted and they were getting money to go home to South Africa. Thinking of what I had read in the papers about the fanatical racism of South Africa and its law of apartheid, I ventured to say, "But things must not be exactly easy for you in South Africa, either."

"That's true," answered one of the Indians, "but they speak our language, and we know what we are up against." In other words, South Africa's way of life, with all its evils, was home to them.

Even so, we can be restless when we are at home, and we can be disturbed by nostalgia for a vanished yesterday or by longings for a utopian tomorrow. The Chinese, I am told, say that there are five points of the compass: North, South, East,

West, and the place where you are. It is the fifth position that is important. We are here in the machine age, urban culture of Western Christendom in its American manifestation in the latter half of the twentieth century. Though we may be restless in it, or even angry with it at times, it is our time and place; it is our home. And it is here that we must take our stand. It is our compass point.

Toward this fairyland of our own native culture it is possible to take any one of three attitudes: *We may embrace it joyously and uncritically. We may despise it. Or we may live within it gratefully, but in creative tension with it.* False prophecy can issue from either of the first two attitudes. To embrace one's culture uncritically is to be false both to your God and to your culture. But to despise it is to be false not only to your own culture but to the God incarnate who entered into the world of culture. The true prophet, therefore, is neither an ardent advocate of the *status quo* nor is he God's angry young man.

ARDENT ADVOCATE OF THE STATUS QUO

First, let us look at the false prophet as advocate of the *status quo*. And let us hasten to say that though his attitude may be false, he has firm ground beneath his feet. He stands upon tradition and upon the positive necessity of conserving the cultural achievements without which we would sink back into animistic primitivism. There is a positive, necessary role for the conservative; and all of us, even those who style ourselves "liberals," are far more conservative than we know.

Again, turn to H. Richard Niebuhr's definition of culture and his enumeration of the chief characteristics of culture. The sixth and last that he mentions is concern with the conservation of values:

Much of the energy which men in their societies expend at any time is given to this complicated task of preserving what they have inherited and made. Their houses, schools, and temples, their roads and machines, stand in constant need of repair. The desert and the jungle threaten every cultivated acre. Even greater are the dangers of decay that surround the less material achievements of the past. The systems of laws and liberties, the customs of social intercourse, the methods of thought, the institutions of learning and religion, the techniques of art, of language, and of morality itself—these cannot be conserved by keeping in repair the walls and documents that are their symbols. They need to be written afresh generation by generation "on the tables of the heart." Let education and training lapse for one generation, and the whole grand structure of past achievements falls into ruin. Culture is social tradition which must be conserved by painful struggle. . . . But whether customs or artifacts are in question, culture cannot be maintained unless men devote a large part of their efforts to the work of conservation.[3]

We in our time have exploded Rousseau's idyllic picture of the noble savage. When a culture breaks or is destroyed it is not the breaking down of prison walls that bar man from returning to Eden. It is the breaking down of the dikes that hold back anarchy, hunger, juvenile delinquency, crime, and revolutionary violence. Thus many people reason, for example, that although Belgium's colonial rule was a violation of the Congo's divine right of self-determination and freedom, it was infinitely better than the rioting, the civil war, the massacres, and the monetary inflation in the Republic of the

[3] *Ibid.*, pp. 37-38.

Congo since it gained independence in 1960. Conservatism has a necessary work to do; and its failure exposes us to demonic perils.

Although the false prophet takes his stand upon the necessary work of conservation that must be done in every culture, he is not a true conservative. He is a reactionary.

Perhaps an illustration will serve to illumine the point. Strolling recently through Cumberland National Forest, I was struck afresh by the large number of fallen trees. A forest is not only a land of the living, it is a cemetery of once living forms which now rot and return to the earth whence they came. A forest is also living trees whose arrow-like trunks pierce the shadowy darkness, straight to the sunlight overhead. That is not all; a forest is fresh every spring, every leaf a chlorophyll factory, a pulsing engine of new life. But most of all a forest is a silent, growing, mighty surge of new life creating new forms, enlarging old forms. If, while walking down a forest trail you stop and hold your breath, you might think that you ought to hear the mighty roar of such an upward Niagara of growing. But the growing is too powerful to be noisy. Even death is not static here; it is the rotting of dead forms which in their dying and rotting create a rich loam, nourishing the living forms at whose roots they lie. A culture is not unlike a forest. It has its living forms, its discarded past, its growing edge, and its pulsing interior life. The true conservative is like a wise forest ranger; but the reactionary, the false prophet, wants to turn it all into a petrified forest and put it in a museum. He views culture in static, not in living, terms; and his devotion is not to its life process but to its symbols and its symptoms.

Narrow Nationalist

When we turn to the Bible and look for ardent spokesmen of the *status quo* we find them in both Testaments. Some of them were narrow nationalists. Among these we would number the historical Jonah, the man who must have furnished the inspiration of the much later Old Testament book bearing his name. From II Kings 14:25 we learn that Jeroboam II "restored the border of Israel from the entrance of Hamath as far as the Sea of Arabah, according to the word of the Lord, the God of Israel, which he spoke by his servant Jonah the son of Amittai, the prophet, who was from Gath-hepher." Jonah thus appears as a prophet of imperialist, military expansion, a man who wrapped himself in his country's flag. And the book bearing his name makes the most of this in portraying him as a one hundred per cent Hebrew who hated Assyrians with a consistently fiery hatred. Narrow nationalists among the prophets were in the majority. When Ahab and Jehoshaphat were planning their military campaign against Syria, their advantage was four hundred to one against Micaiah (I Kings 22:1-28).

It is only from across the border that narrow nationalism looks ugly. On our side of the border it is red-blooded patriotism; across the border it appears as chauvinistic hatred, as warmongering and saber rattling; paranoid suspicion on a mass scale. Nowhere does nationalism appear in a more demonic light than in the book of Revelation. Take this flaming passage from Rev. 19:17-20:

Then I saw an angel standing in the sun, and with a loud voice he called to all the birds that fly in mid-heaven, "Come, gather for the great supper of God, to eat the flesh of kings, the flesh of captains, the flesh of mighty men, the flesh of horses and their riders, and the flesh of all men, both free and slave, both small and great." And I saw the beast and the kings of the earth with their armies gathered to make war against him who sits upon the horse and against his army. And the beast was captured, and with it the false prophet who in its presence had worked the signs by which he deceived those who had received the mark of the beast and who worshiped its image. These two were thrown alive into the lake of fire that burns with brimstone.

The church, under the cross of persecution and martyrdom, had to call Rome a beast and emperor worship his false prophet. The Jews in World War II had to do the same with Hitler. But the issue is not often so sharply drawn. Church and state do not always stand facing each other, drawn up for battle. More often they live in peaceful alliance. Caesar is a king with smiles, conferring benefits such as tax-exemptions upon the churches and the institutions of the churches. For this we sing, "God bless America, land that I love." Our hearts stir with honest patriotism; in actual practice it is hard to tell where the feelings of patriotism leave off and the emotions of religion begin; they commingle so easily. It is easy to say with our lips, "Honor all men. Love the brotherhood. Fear God. Honor the emperor" (I Pet. 2:17), but in actual practice it is easier to pay reverent fear to the emperor—that is, the state—and to accord God the lower place of secondary and instrumental honor. Love of country tends to overshadow love of God in all people. To that extent we are subject to the temptations of false prophecy; and to the extent that we succumb we are John the Baptist to the Mussolinis, the Stalins, the Hitlers of the world who have made of the totalitarian state the "satanic manifestation of our time." The false prophet may be a narrow nationalist.

Status Seekers

He may also be a *status seeker*. We do not have a good contemporary name for him, but his biblical counterpart is found in the prophets of Baal. They appear in Jeremiah's indictment against false leaders:

> The priests did not say, "Where is the Lord?"
>   Those who handle the law did not know me;
> the rulers transgressed against me;
>   *the prophets prophesied by Baal,*
>   *and went after the things that do not profit.*
>   (Jer. 2:8, italics mine.)

The Baalim in ancient Palestine were local nature gods or lords, whose main function was to bring fertility to the soil and prosperity to the people. They were worshiped in hilltop shrines through rites of sympathetic magic which included cult prostitution. That is to say, they were gods of property, prosperity, and sex. Since the Canaanites who worshiped the Baalim were more prosperous than the Israelites, possessed the most fertile parts of the country, and lived in fine walled cities, going after Baal from the Israelite standpoint also meant striving for a higher status. The prophet of Baal, therefore, is spokesman of the values of property, prosperity, sex, and status seeking. The fertility rites of the Canaanitish shrines should not utterly surprise us. The alliance of sex with prosperity, the exploitation of sex for the sake of prosperity, has its modern counterparts. In fact, sometimes it appears that modern advertising is an elaborate fertility rite, using sex appeal to stimulate sales.

According to Gibson Winter, in *The Suburban Captivity of*

the Churches, much of our suburban Christianity is prophesying by this Baal of property, prosperity, and status seeking. The preacher in such a church becomes the minister in the gray flannel suit. God calls him not where the harvest is ripest, but where the grass is greenest—where the biggest salary, the nicest parsonage, the biggest church, and the richest people are. When a minister begins to pursue prestige and luxury he begins to prophesy by Baal. It is difficult, even for a man of God, to live in an affluent society without becoming a man of the world. Then the genuine, prophetic function goes out of the ministry, and the minister becomes the twentieth-century counterpart of the town crier, mounting the pulpit every Sunday morning and calling out, "Eleven o'clock, and all is well!" He cries " 'Peace,' when there is no peace." He soothes and solaces when he ought to disturb; he condones when he ought to judge and forgive. The false prophet may be a prophet of Baal.

Sadducee

Again, the false prophet may be a Sadducee. Jesus warned his disciples more than once, "Beware of the leaven of the Pharisees and Sadducees" (Matt. 16:6, 11). Ignoring for the time being the leaven of the Pharisees, consider the leaven of the Sadducees. Who were the Sadducees? To put the answer in the bluntest terms, they were Jews who collaborated with the hated Roman overlords of Palestine. They had power, prestige, and wealth—all of it dependent upon their ability to serve and appease their Roman masters, and to keep the people beneath them quiet and subservient. Their motto was, "Don't rock the boat."

The Sadducees feared that Jesus would disturb the *status*

quo which treated them so well. They saw him as a threat to their vested interest:

So the chief priests [Sadducees] and the Pharisees gathered the council, and said, "What are we to do? For this man performs many signs. If we let him go on thus, every one will believe in him, and the Romans will come and destroy both our holy place and our nation." But one of them, Caiaphas, who was high priest that year, said to them, "You know nothing at all; you do not understand that it is expedient for you that one man should die for the people, and that the whole nation should not perish" (John 11:47-50).

The thing that disturbs any *status quo* which holds large masses of people in some kind of bondage is to let Jesus go on speaking. Where his voice is heard there is danger that deep social wrongs will be righted, that ancient evils will be overturned, and that those who hold places of power and privilege will be unseated.

It is not farfetched to think of the minister as a Sadducee in this sense. A minister normally has an entree into polite society which others gain only if they are rich or wellborn. He may like to think of himself as the spokesman of God, but in very human terms he is the hireling of the congregation; they hired him; they can fire him. And if he treads too rudely on local prejudices, they will fire him, and he knows it. In such a situation, that fatal disease, the silence of the pulpit, sets in. For the sake of peace and concord—and for the sake of job-insurance—the minister in his warm ecclesiastical nest decides, like Caiaphas, "that it is expedient . . . that one man should die," rather than that his highly beneficial leadership in this congregation should be terminated. The weapon with which he assassinates Christ is neither cross, nor spear, nor firing squad nor gas chamber. It is the lethal bludgeon of his silence. Hence against the background of racial crisis the minister whose other name is Caiaphas preaches on the lilies of the field and the sins of Red China. But in this place where he is, and to his own situation, Jesus is never permitted to speak. Sabapathy Kulandran, an Indian who spent four years in America, wrote a devastating book, *The Message and the Silence of the American Pulpit.* The thing that shocked this Asian Christian was not what we ministers are saying, but our failure to speak when a word from the Lord is urgently needed. "Beware of the leaven of the Sadducees."

GOD'S ANGRY MAN

The true prophet is not an ardent advocate of the *status quo.* But neither is he God's angry man. Times of massive transition are also times of massive anger. For then the cultural earth changes as in earthquake, cultural mountains crumble into the sea, the seas roar and foam, and a great fear assails the hearts of men. Then fear gives birth to smoldering resentment or blazing hostility. Times of cultural earthquake are times of massive anger. If we could gather all the resentment, hostility, and hatred from two hundred million American hearts into a mass and transport it in a giant asbestos vehicle to some isolated landscape in the great western desert, it would blaze with the fury of an inferno. Such anger breaks out in many places under many guises.

Hatred of Current Culture

It may appear as hatred of current culture. Its biblical symbol is Jonah sitting in petulance and anger in a hermit's booth out-

43

side Nineveh, waiting for God to destroy the hated Assyrian capital. Or it is Elijah under the juniper tree and in the cave of Horeb, pitying himself: "I have been very jealous for the Lord, the God of hosts; for the people of Israel have forsaken thy covenant, thrown down thy altars, and slain thy prophets with the sword; and I, even I only, am left; and they seek my life, to take it away" (I Kings 19:14).

Fortunately Elijah's withdrawal and his self-pity were only temporary. But with some people it is a permanent state of mind. There are hermit huts, anchorite caves, ascetic's pillars enough to attest to it. The Dead Sea scrolls have recently brought to light the Qumran Community which retired from the culture of Judaism in Hellenic-Roman times to the arid wastes overlooking the Dead Sea. This motif of permanent withdrawal runs deep in human history and it flows from ancient days straight through the medieval era into modern times. The solidly built halls and massive buildings of Shakertown, Kentucky, only a few miles from Lexington, remind us that Protestantism, as well as Roman and Orthodox Catholicism, has had its own forms of monasticism. Janice Holt Giles has told the tense, heartbreaking story of the Shaker withdrawal in her book *The Believers.*

The hatred of current culture also comes to light in non-ecclesiastical guise. The English poet Stephen Spender finds contemporary writing characterized by nostalgia and hatred:

A poet not only feels that he belongs to the company of those whose conversation is poetry, but he may envy them the culture which made them happier than he feels in the age of mass-cult and advertising. Hence the paradox of the extraordinary hatred of modern life which is characteristic of the writing which at the same time is itself modern. . . .

44

Poets learned a modern language, invented a modern idiom, in order to express an extreme hatred for the modern world, an overwhelming nostalgia for the past.[4]

Spender goes on to say that the earlier modern writers, such as T. S. Eliot, James Joyce, and Ezra Pound, are characterized by a hatred of the modern world based on nostalgia for a vanished past. But, he says, the new generation of modern writers which has emerged since World War II has no past to be nostalgic about, and these writers tend to concentrate all their emotion in hatred and despair. To continue, Spender writes:

It seems to me that a real difference between generations—far greater than the usual Beatnik and Espresso Bar ones that are named—is that the post-World War II generation does not feel nostalgic. By this, I mean that they do not lead interior mental lives in which they feel themselves time's exiles because they were not born in the Renaissance or into an "organic community." [5]

Spender concludes with the conviction that hatred and despair of the modern world are nihilistic of literature itself. "Modern literature has to see the good as well as the bad in the modern world if there is to be a future for literature at all." [5] Ironically, the false prophet who despises his own culture does not deliver himself from it but perishes with it. His hatred is a chain that makes him captive to it.

Heresy Hunter

God's angry man may appear as a heresy hunter, a detective of conspiracies, a witch burner. He is a more intense kin of

[4] Stephen Spender, "What Modern Writers Forget," *Saturday Review* (January 20, 1962), pp. 16-17.
[5] *Ibid.*, pp. 33, 34.

the man we have just been describing. He sees himself and his beloved way of life ringed by enemies, infiltrated by subversives. In this time of massive social transition, things are out of joint and, to his mind, that could not be because the culture is leaving its chambered past for larger mansions, or because of impersonal forces released by, but not entirely controlled by, a scientific and technological age. No. It is far more simple than that. Things are wrong; this angry man feels that somebody is guilty of conspiring to harm us by deliberate intent.

This zealot is sure that there is a conspirator, but he has great difficulty in identifying him, as witness the fact that the prophets, priests, and princes of Judah supposed Jeremiah to be the most dangerous subversive of seventh-century Jerusalem. After Jeremiah's stirring temple sermon (Jer. 7, 26), he was branded a national enemy. Then the priests and the prophets said to the princes and to all the people, "This man deserves the sentence of death, because he has prophesied against this city" (Jer. 26:11). In the light of later centuries it can be seen that the real enemies of Judah were the abuses that Jeremiah sought to reform.

This accusatory mentality appears in our time in the form of the radical right—the John Birchers, the White Citizens' Council, the Black Muslims, the American Nazi Party, and many more. Their profile is deftly sketched by Mark Sherwin in an important book, *The Extremists.*

Notice, for example, Robert Welch's identification of the enemy in the following paragraph from his pen:

The Communists can now use all the power and prestige of the Presidency of the United States to implement their plans, just as fully and openly as they dare. They have arrived at this point by three stages. In the first stage, Roosevelt thought he was using the Communists to promote his personal ambitions and grandiose schemes. Of course, instead, the Communists were using him; but without his knowledge or understanding of his place in their game. In the second stage, Truman was used by the Communists, with his knowledge and acquiescence, as the price he consciously paid for their making him President. In the third stage, in my own firm opinion, the Communists have one of their own actually in the Presidency. For this third man, Eisenhower, there is only one possible word to describe his purposes and his actions. The word is "treason." [6]

Curiously enough, the answer to these reckless allegations of Robert Welch and his John Birch Society came from the *Literary Gazette* of Moscow. The issue of April 4, 1961, said:

The predictions of Lenin are materializing in the United States. Lenin said that the most ardent foes of Communism will eventually become frightened and suspicious of anybody who does not agree with them. . . . Several years ago an American Senator by the name of McCarthy performed a great service for world Communism . . . by throwing suspicion of Communist affiliation on some very important personalities of the capitalist world. Instead of harming, he actually strengthened the Communist party in the United States. Now the Communist movement has gained unexpectedly a new supporter. His name is Robert Welch. [7]

It seems hardly likely that many ministers will jump on the bandwagon of the radical right or become zealots in its cause, though some have done so. The temptation of false prophecy is usually more subtle. It is to ride the coattails of reaction by

---

[6] Mark Sherwin, *The Extremists* (New York: St. Martin's Press, 1963), pp. 47-48.
[7] *Ibid.*, p. 81.

attacking communism and un-Americanism in loud but vague generalities. Such a blunderbuss attack inflicts no wounds on communism or un-Americanism, but it is good for a popular following in the United States among certain fanatical zealots. It is hard to refrain from flagellating the current, popular whipping boy; and it is even more difficult to get down to the concrete task of intelligent social salvation. It would seem to be a reliable rule that preachers should remove from their pulpit vocabularies all words ending in "ism." These are words that stir emotions, but do little in the building of a better world; and they may do great harm.

As was said earlier in this chapter, toward our own native culture it is possible to take any one of three attitudes: We may embrace it joyously and uncritically. We may despise it in its current manifestations. (These are the alternatives of the false prophet.) Or, as a third alternative, we may live within our culture gratefully, but in creative tension with it. This third alternative may be tersely characterized by Robert Frost's suggestion for his own epitaph:

> And were an epitaph to be my story
> I'd have a short one ready for my own.
> I would have written of me on my stone:
> I had a lover's quarrel with the world.[8]

---

[8] From "The Lesson for Today" from *Complete Poems of Robert Frost.* Copyright 1942 by Robert Frost. Reprinted by permission of Holt, Rinehart and Winston, Inc.

Trapped in the Temple

The temple sermon of Jeremiah (Jer. 7, 26) was a radical sermon. If it were spoken today, some would say that it was communist-inspired. "Thus says the Lord: If you will not listen to me, to walk in my law which I have set before you, and to heed the words of my servants the prophets whom I send to you urgently, though you have not heeded, then I will make this house like Shiloh, and I will make this city a curse for all the nations of the earth" (Jer. 26:4-6).

In saying this, Jeremiah was only reechoing the century-old prophecy of Micah:

> Hear this, you heads of the house of Jacob
>   and rulers of the house of Israel,
>   who abhor justice
>   and pervert all equity,
>   who build Zion with blood
>   and Jerusalem with wrong.
> Its heads give judgment for a bribe,
>   its priests teach for hire,
>   its prophets divine for money;

> yet they lean upon the Lord and say,
>> "Is not the Lord in the midst of us?
>> No evil shall come upon us."
> Therefore because of you
>> Zion shall be plowed as a field;
> Jerusalem shall become a heap of ruins,
>> and the mountain of the house a wooded height
>>> (Mic. 3:9-12).

Such fiery words, belching like a blast from a flamethrower into the sacred precincts of the temple, were dangerous to the man who spoke them. Just how dangerous is seen from the fate of Uriah of Kiriath-jearim: "He prophesied against this city and against this land in words like those of Jeremiah. And when King Jehoiakim, with all his warriors and all the princes, heard his words, the king sought to put him to death; but when Uriah heard it, he was afraid and fled and escaped to Egypt. Then King Jehoiakim sent to Egypt certain men . . . and they fetched Uriah from Egypt and brought him to King Jehoiakim, who slew him with the sword and cast his dead body into the burial place of the common people" (Jer. 26:20-23).

The full impact of Jeremiah's temple sermon does not hit us until we translate it into modern terms. It is as if a Roman Catholic priest standing before the altar of the High Mass said to a Sunday morning congregation of Roman Catholics, "God is going to smash the Vatican, the seat of the Vicar of Christ on earth, and reduce it to a heap of smouldering ruins." Or, to bring it still closer home, it is like a Protestant minister's blazing word of doom from the pulpit of his church:

We have a hymn which we sing in this congregation. It contains these words:

50

> I love thy Church, O God!
> Her walls before thee stand,
> Dear as the apple of thine eye,
> And graven on thy hand.

Words like these can lull us into a false spiritual security. The church—this church—is not always the apple of God's eye. There are times when God does not have a good word to say for the churches. There have been times in the past when he has said, and he may now be saying to the churches: "I hate, I despise your Easter festivals and your Communion services, and I take no delight in your solemn assemblies." (See Amos 5:21.) God is not always pleased with his church. Although he can sometimes use it as the ready instrument in his hands with which to do his work in the world, there are other times, and this is one of them, when it is an offense to him, an obstruction, and he must clear it out of his path. Hear the words of First Peter: "For the time has come for judgment to begin with the household of God" (I Pet. 4:17). Picture the judgment of God falling like a hydrogen bomb upon the world. The church is not beyond its range, "safe and secure from all alarms." On the contrary, the church is at the center of the target area, in the very hottest heat of the fire.

In this seventh decade of the twentieth century, such a sermon is inconceivable. We are not really so unlike the cultic prophets of ancient Israel who took their living from the temple and who drifted into the belief that God also took his living from the temple. Faced by the fiery judgment of God in the wars and revolutions of their days, the prophets of ancient times could not see these disturbances as the work of God. They felt that they were keeping God safe in the Holy of Holies, as they were keeping themselves secure in the temple precincts. Hence it came about that in the crisis of their times, when men needed to be turned inside out by a radical repentance, they had no word of God to speak, but only a hollow

51

word of their own echoing in the emptiness of the Holy Place: "The temple of the Lord, the temple of the Lord, the temple of the Lord" (Jer. 7:4).

We even know the names of some of those false prophets: There was Hananiah the prophet of Gibeon, where the sun had stood still in the day of Joshua; he was trying to make history stand still. His story is told in Jeremiah, chapter 28. There were also Ahab the son of Kolaiah, Zedekiah the son of Maaseiah and Shemaiah of Nehelam, all operating from Babylon after the first captivity but before the destruction of the temple. Their story appears in Jer. 29. Hananiah had many colleagues; Jeremiah stood alone. The false prophets were in the majority, but they were trapped by the temple.

How did the false prophets come to be thus bound by the cultus, thus trapped in the temple? The answer to that question will do more than answer our curiosity about ancient history. It will also become a contemporary signal of warning. The answer, as unfolded in what follows, may be summarized briefly: "professionalism," "pigeonholing," and "cheap grace and easy merit."

PROFESSIONALISM

Old Testament scholars now tell us that the professionals of the temple included not only priests and Levites but prophets as well. And the distinction between priests and prophets, so sharp a generation ago to biblical scholars, has proved to be largely false. Both priest and prophet derived their living from the temple offerings.

As a minister it has at times sobered me to realize that my salary was first presented at the altar in an offering to God.

The dollar that I spend for my groceries on Saturday was first placed on an offering plate and presented to God, the previous Lord's Day. That dime I put into the coffee machine was first of all a part of an offering in a service of worship.

This simple fact of economic dependence upon the religious institution may easily warp my perspective. Paul, supporting himself by the work of his hands as a weaver of goat's hair into tents, sails, and overcoats, would have said, "For me, to *make a living* is tentmaking; but for me, to *live* is Christ." With me, the two—life and living—coalesce. The institutional church bearing the name of Christ is my living, whether or not Christ is my life. Herein lies one danger of false prophecy.

The connection between the church offering and the prophet's living may not be as apparent to us now as it was a few years ago in some rural congregations and as it still is in some mission lands. Filipino pastors today in outlying *barrios* or villages are apt to receive a part of their salaries in *pesos* and the rest in rice with perhaps a chicken or two thrown in. But the rice and the chickens are first presented to God at the altar. The connection between the offering and the minister's living is obvious.

It was hardly less so in the first student-pastorate that I served as an undergraduate ministerial student in Bethany College. Every Saturday noon I boarded the bus for Wellsburg, West Virginia, where I caught a train for Wheeling. Walking from the Pennsylvania Railway Station to the Baltimore and Ohio, I then caught a four o'clock train to New Martinsville; at New Martinsville I changed to the "shortline," and arrived at Pine Grove, Wetzel County, West Virginia, at seven o'clock that evening. On Monday morning I repeated the journey in reverse, arriving in Bethany early in the afternoon. But I did not return as I had gone. When I went down on Saturday I usually had barely enough cash to pay the train fare. Coming back, my pockets were loaded with fifteen dollars worth of pennies, nickels, dimes, and quarters. That was my "priest's portion" of the Sunday offerings.

In those days I was engaged to be married, and my fiancée (who is now my wife) decided that we should save all our pennies toward our first set of silverware. Most of "our" pennies came out of my pocket, and each week they lightened the load considerably. In fact, it took only a little more than a year to save up fifteen dollars exclusively from pennies, nearly all of which had come through the offerings of the Pine Grove Christian Church. We are still eating with that silverware. Now, as I pick up a knife or fork from that set, I think, "Once you were copper; but now, through the blessings of Elder Stackpole, you have become silver in the mouth of a preacher."

I am speaking lightly. When confronting a matter like this, one dares not become too serious, or the thought would strike him to death. For, ever since the beginning of those weekend trips many years ago, most of my salary first went into an offering plate, and some elder or minister prayed over it, asking God to bless it toward the building of his kingdom.

"And this shall be the priests' due from the people, from those offering a sacrifice, whether it be ox or sheep: they shall give to the priest the shoulder" (Deut. 18:3). The practice of giving the priest the right shoulder of an ox or sheep seems to have gone back to pre-Hebrew Canaan. Archaeologists, in fact, uncovered a late bronze age Canaanite temple at Lachish and found there a pit filled with right shoulder bones. The

54

number of shoulder bones in that pit stands as a symbol of the professional religionist's vested interest in the ongoing life of the religious institution.

It is not merely that we take our living economically from the church institution. We also take our success from it. A young minister recently appeared on television. After the young minister had been introduced, he was asked the question that the world asks, and that ministers frequently ask themselves: "Do you have a big church?" It was with a visible letdown that he answered, "No, I'm afraid I have a very small church." But, just as obviously, he wanted it to be a big church —so that it could become the stairway to the stars of his personal glory.

Now consider the harvest of consequences: Instead of fastening his compassionate eye upon the people of the lonely crowd who are under his care, that minister puts the church as institution at center. The chief end of "his" church members is to serve the church—that is to say, to swell its treasury, to expand its membership roll, to build for it new buildings, to make it a beehive of activities, to gain recognition for it in the community and in his denomination. The chief end of these church members is to serve the institution; and the chief function of God is to preserve it.

In my position as a teacher of homiletics it has been my task for the past seventeen years to read and listen to hundreds of sermons by young seminarians on the threshold or in the early years of their ministry. One of the comments that I have had to write on sermon outlines and manuscripts perhaps more frequently than any other is "institution-centered." And the next comment, which is twin to the other, is, "You are punishing your people." Why? Because a minister who is centered upon the church as an institution, and who in consequence begins to use people to advance the success of the institution, soon comes to look upon people not as persons who need love but as troublesome obstacles who must be cleared out of his path or as slow-moving beasts who must be driven. Pastoral concern turns into executive efficiency; and when efficiency is thwarted, as it almost inevitably must be, ministerial energy is consumed in frustration and anger. And it flares out as punishment.

It is true that the full spectrum of God's Word includes a note of judgment and that without it there can be no salvation. But there is a vast difference between judgment and punishment. The judgment of God issues from his love. It warns the sinner in order to win him to a new life. But the punishment of a minister issues from his anxiety and from his anger. It tries to coerce the sinner, not for the sake of the sinner but for the sake of something organizational and impersonal. It becomes a kind of exploitation.

It is true that the church must have an institution, but it must never be made to exist for the sake of the institution. On the contrary, the institution must exist to serve as the channel of God's redemptive concern for people and as an instrument through which the communion of saints becomes a reality.

Toward the closing months of World War II the Nazis devised a stratagem which might have proved more damaging to the Allied cause than the blitzing of London. They manufactured millions of dollars in counterfeit Allied currency, so skillfully engraved and printed that it would have fooled even the experts. The war ended only a few days before the false money was to have been put into circulation. It is well for us to remember that Satan does his best work in the church

56

not by declaring open war, but through cleverly devised counterfeits. Chief among these are institutionalism, a counterfeit for churchmanship; and punishment, a counterfeit for the judgment of God.

PIGEONHOLING

Closely allied to professionalism is pigeonholing. It is a common consequence of institutionalism. The empty echo of the verbal circle in Jeremiah's temple sermon expresses it: "The temple of the Lord, the temple of the Lord, the temple of the Lord." It is as a word trapped in the temple, bouncing from wall to wall within it, but never escaping as God's messenger into the outside world.

Every religious institution comes with a built-in tension between the localization of God and his universal lordship. If we are to acknowledge that

> The earth is the Lord's and the fulness thereof,
> the world and those who dwell therein (Ps. 24:1)

and that all our times are in his hand (Ps. 31:15), we must do so in a designated place and at an appointed hour. But as soon as God is given a sacred day and a sacred hour, there is the danger that all other days and hours will become secular. And as soon as God is given a sacred house, there is the danger that he will be placed under house arrest. We began by giving God one holy day and one sacred hour so as to be reminded that all days are holy, all hours sacred; we end by shutting God out of all days but the Sabbath, out of all hours but the hour of prayer. We began by giving God a house so as to be reminded that the whole earth is his dwelling place; we end by confining God to that temple, so as to take the world outside its holy courts into our own control.

The words of Solomon at the dedication of the temple reflect this tension. On the one hand there is the omnipresence of God, heard in Solomon's prayer, "But will God indeed dwell on the earth? Behold, heaven and the highest heaven cannot contain thee; how much less this house which I have built!" (I Kings 8:27). On the other hand, there is the localization of God. We find Solomon building a temple on the heights of Jerusalem, providing within it an unlighted room thirty feet square—a Holy of Holies—where God might dwell in thick darkness:

> The Lord has set the sun in the heavens,
> but has said that he would dwell in thick darkness.
> I have built thee an exalted house,
> a place for thee to dwell in for ever (I Kings 8:12-13).

The pigeonholing of God probably is rooted in our fear of him, and our fear is rooted in our disobedience and rebellion. Adam and Eve hid themselves from God among the trees of the garden. With the advance of civilization we have improved upon Adam. We do not hide from God; we conceal him within the dark recesses of the temple and shut him off with strong walls so that he will not break forth to endanger our common life. We have provided a ghetto for God; we have segregated him.

The pigeonholing of God becomes possible, paradoxically, only when the religious institution is thriving. When I came to Lexington nearly seventeen years ago, Everybody's Church was meeting for worship and study on Sunday mornings in the Ben Ali Theater. I remember preaching there one Sunday morning when the minister was on vacation. With garish colored lights shining in my eyes, with stage trappings all around me and the congregation occupying dimly lighted theater seats like an audience waiting for the performance to begin, I experienced the almost total absence of what we have come to call "the atmosphere of worship." (How frequently we confuse "atmosphere" with a carefully contrived physical setting, which is nothing more than good ecclesiastical theater!) "Scotty" Cowan, who was the minister of Everybody's Church in those days, used to point out the virtues of his situation. There was no danger, he said, that his people would confuse church with the theater building; and the church, if it had any existence at all during the week, had to be where it ought to be—out among the people. There was little institution, therefore little temptation to put God in a pigeonhole.

Most of our church life stands in sharp contrast to that. We have an imposing church building and a thriving program of activities going on within it. It is here that the danger lies. A minister of my acquaintance says that he makes a point of never using the word *church* for the building; he calls that a *chapel,* thus making it clear that *church* can refer only to people. It is a practice to be commended. Sören Kierkegaard wrote in this connection:

We have what one might call a complete inventory of churches, bells, organs, benches, alms-boxes, foot-warmers, tables, hearses, etc. But when Christianity does not exist, the existence of this inventory, so far from being . . . an advantage, is far rather a peril, because it is so infinitely likely to give rise to a false im-

59

pression and the false inference that when we have such a complete Christian inventory we must of course have Christianity, too.[1]

As soon as we begin to confuse church with church building and religion with the activities that go on within the church building, we are genuinely trapped in the temple. A meal eaten on the church premises is not necessarily any more religious than a meal eaten in a cafeteria or at the Kiwanis. A committee meeting in the church building is not necessarily less secular than a meeting of the greens committee at the country club.

Much church activity falls short of being genuinely Christian because it is self-regarding activity, activity for activity's sake, uninformed by gospel, scripturally illiterate and content to remain so—sacramentally shallow, hollow of the spirit or reality of prayer, and devoid of concern or compassion within or without the fellowship.

To the extent that the church exists within a community not to serve but to be served, not to lose its life for Christ's sake but to preserve it and even to enhance it; to the extent that the church exists as a spiritual lobby, a religious pressure group for the benefit of those who have a vested interest in religion; to that extent it has tried to pigeonhole God and to make his word of no effect. This is what secularization is—the pigeonholing of God in the religious institution. Or, to use the words of Peter Berger in *The Noise of Solemn Assemblies*, secularization is the "segregation of religious motives within the religious institution itself. Within the broad areas of political,

[1] Kierkegaard, *Attack Upon Christendom*, trans. Walter Lowrie (Princeton: Princeton University Press, 1944), p. 30.

economic, and social life, religious motives appear to be of little relevance." [2] We thus confront the paradox of a thriving religious establishment in a highly secular society. The more thriving the church is, the more secular society becomes.

There seems to be no cure of this malady short of daily facing the great God of the whole world. With Solomon we need always to pray, especially in church, "Behold, heaven and the highest heaven cannot contain thee; how much less this house which I have built!" With the Apostle Paul, we need to say, "The God who made the world and everything in it, being Lord of heaven and earth, does not live in shrines made by man, nor is he served by human hands, as though he needed anything, since he himself gives to all men life and breath and everything" (Acts 17:24-25).

CHEAP GRACE AND EASY MERIT

The false prophet and those whom he beguiles are trapped in the temple, victims of the *professionalism* and *pigeonholing* that arise from undue emphasis upon the religious institution. If we look again at Jeremiah's temple sermon we will see a third way in which the temple trapped his contemporaries— a way in which it may also trap us. We may call this peril *cheap grace and easy merit.*

Cheap grace showed itself in the time of Jeremiah, as it shows itself today, in three ways: as *salvation by ritual,* as *justification by membership,* and as *forgiveness without repentance.*

[2] Peter L. Berger, *The Noise of Solemn Assemblies* (Garden City: Doubleday & Company, 1961), p. 34.

Salvation by Ritual

Jeremiah's words about *salvation by ritual* flame up from the page:

Behold, you trust in deceptive words to no avail. Will you steal, murder, commit adultery, swear falsely, burn incense to Baal, and go after other gods that you have not known, and then come and stand before me in this house, which is called by my name, and say, "We are delivered!"—only to go on doing all these abominations? (Jer. 7:8-10).

Ritual, dissociated from everyday life, is supposed to set people at rights with God. It seems that God likes anthems, hymns, prayers, and sermons; that God takes deep satisfaction from sacrifices and sacred meals eaten in his house. Why God should like these things remains to us a mystery; but if he wants them, we will be generous and do him the favor of giving them to him, not once in a lifetime but once every week, on schedule. The Lord knows that we are bored most of the time we are in church, but he will also notice with what patience and perseverance we endure that boredom. We take our punishment manfully. And all of this will be registered in heaven on the credit side of our ledger. Can you think of any easier way of acquiring merit?

Religious ritual dissociated from everyday life, offered as appeasement to God—that is painless therapy. The human race has always been attracted to it. And false prophets have always offered it. Jeremiah indicts them for it:

> They have healed the wound of my people lightly,
>   saying, "Peace, Peace,"
> when there is no peace (Jer. 8:11).

This is placing poultices on wounds needing deep surgery.

Ritual has its place, not because God needs it, but because man does. Ritual is needed not in isolation from everyday life, but as a symbolic aid to lifting up all of life "as a living sacrifice, holy and acceptable to God," which is the only acceptable service (Rom. 12:1). As soon as ritual is cut off from such a living sacrifice, it offers neither grace nor merit; on the contrary, it becomes an abomination.

The major prophets were never in doubt about that: Jeremiah as God's spokesman said,

Add your burnt offerings to your sacrifices, and eat the flesh. For in the day that I brought them out of the land of Egypt, I did not speak to your fathers or command them concerning burnt offerings and sacrifices. But this command I gave them, "Obey my voice, and I will be your God, and you shall be my people; and walk in all the way that I command you, that it may be well with you" (Jer. 7:21-23).

A hundred years earlier Isaiah was even more vehement as he hurled the Word of God into the temple:

When you come to appear before me,
    who requires of you
    this trampling of my courts?
Bring no more vain offerings;
    incense is an abomination to me.
New moon and sabbath and the calling of assemblies—
    I cannot endure iniquity and the solemn assembly.
Your new moons and your appointed feasts
    my soul hates;
they have become a burden to me,
    I am weary of bearing them.

63

> When you spread forth your hands,
>   I will hide my eyes from you;
> even though you make many prayers,
>   I will not listen;
>   your hands are full of blood (Isa. 1:12-15).

Amos spoke the same theme in blistering words, as did other prophets. False prophets promise salvation by ritual; they offer peace by pills and poultices. Genuine prophets call for deep surgery.

Justification by Membership

Closely akin to salvation by ritual is *justification by membership*. This comes about as a rather natural perversion of the covenant. The Israelites were God's chosen people, as Christians, under the new covenant, are also God's chosen people—an elect race, a royal priesthood, God's holy nation. Chosen for what? Chosen to suffer and to serve for all humanity. However, it is uncomfortably demanding to read the covenant in that light. Members of the New Israel as of the Old Israel have preferred to believe that they were chosen as God's pets with special privileges and immunities.

This is the opposite of guilt by association. It is innocence by association, acquittal by belonging to the right people. It makes church membership a form of snobbery, not unlike the snobbishness of the blue-blooded, socially elite. Among the Israelites in ancient times it took the form of a boast, "We are the sons of Abraham." To this Jeremiah answered that they might be Abraham's physical descendants but that spiritually they were no relation. Circumcised in the flesh, they were not circumcised of heart (Jer. 4:4).

This prophetic insight was absorbed into the spirit of John

the Baptist and poured itself out upon the Pharisees and
Sadducees in scorching words:

You brood of vipers! Who warned you to flee from the wrath
to come? Bear fruit that befits repentance, and do not presume to
yourselves, "We have Abraham as our father"; for I tell you, God
is able from these stones to raise up children to Abraham. Even
now the ax is laid to the root of the trees; every tree therefore
that does not bear good fruit is cut down and thrown into the fire
(Matt. 3:7-10).

To be among God's chosen people is not to be exempt from
his moral requirements; it is not to inherit special privileges
and immunities. It is to take up a special task, to undergo
vicarious sufferings. More than that, it is to stand under the
severity of a special judgment. Amos spoke for all the
prophets:

> You only have I known
>   of all the families of the earth;
> therefore [notice the surprising consequence!]
>   I will punish you
>   for all your iniquities (Amos 3:2).

And Peter spoke for all the apostles: "For the time has come
for judgment to begin with the household of God" (I Pet.
4:17). As for the prophets and teachers—who may be tempted
to think of themselves as an elite among the privileged, with
special immunities all their own—the word of James is even
more uncomfortable: "Let not many of you become teachers,
my brethren, for you know that we who teach shall be judged
with greater strictness" (Jas. 3:1). There is no justification by
mere membership.

Forgiveness Without Repentance

Both salvation by ritual and justification by membership are special forms of cheap grace and easy merit which participate in an even wider misconception—that of *forgiveness without repentance*. This is what we mean fundamentally by cheap grace. It substitutes the condoning of sin for the forgiveness of sin. It is forgiveness without cost to God or man; therefore it is "forgiveness" that changes nothing in God or man. It is the kind of grace called for in the celebrated cynical remark of Heinrich Heine: "Certainly he [God] will forgive me; that's his business."

It is popular just now to speak harshly of "moralism." By moralism is meant a religion of ethical duty and social reform undertaken in the spirit of the Pharisees and Puritans. It is bad Christianity. It is bad, however, not because it calls for moral uprightness and social justice, but because it has the wrong rootage in duty—self-justification and loveless judgment of others. It is bad also because it bears the wrong fruit —self-righteousness or despair. Moralism is an attempt at salvation by human merit; that is to say, it is "salvation" without a savior.

Cheap grace seeks to dispense with such moralism, but it does so by attempting to bypass judgment. Cheap grace is not moralistic; it is worse than moralistic. It is libertine. For the meeting between God and man takes place in earnest only when man meets God as the righteous judge. It is guilty Cain hearing God's question, "Where is Abel your brother?" It is runaway Jacob at the fords of the Jabbok, wrestling all night with an angel and an uneasy conscience. It is Saul of Tarsus on the Damascus Road struck blind and listening to a voice that asks, "Saul, Saul, why do you persecute me?"

Let us never try to turn grace into a gimmick for bypassing God's lofty moral requirements. In a recent chapter on hermeneutics in his book *Word and Faith,* Gerhard Ebeling summarizes all principles for hearing the Word of God speaking to us through the Bible in a single, simple formula: "With an eye to the real sphere of the word-event I suggest for consideration the formula: the hermeneutic principle is *man as conscience.*" [3]

This principle he later elaborates in the same volume:

To answer for (*verantworten*) God before the world means: to let God and the world come together by means of "word" (*das Wort*). Only so will man be affected by our talk of God. And the only responsible talk of God is that which aims at the place where God and the world meet as it were in a mathematical point. That place is the conscience. Because responsible talk of God aims at the conscience, the world necessarily also becomes a question when talk of God stands in question. For conscience sake we cannot speak of God without speaking of the world. For as conscience man stands between God and the world. What is real in our talk of God comes to light in how that talk of God is related to the world. [4]

This means that a man begins to hear what God has to say to him as a person through the Bible when he approaches the Bible as one who stands under the moral judgment of God—as one who through disobedience has learned in the Eden

---

[3] Gerhard Ebeling, *Word and Faith,* trans. James W. Leitch (Philadelphia: Fortress Press, 1963), p. 332.

[4] *Ibid.,* p. 356.

of his own life to make the distinction between right and wrong.

When we come into the presence of Christ we must come only as those whom the law has condemned. We must come in penitence. It is for this reason that cheap grace is such a blasphemy. What is cheap grace? Perhaps no one ever explained it more clearly than the young German martyr, Dietrich Bonhoeffer:

Cheap grace is the preaching of forgiveness without requiring repentance, baptism without church discipline, Communion without confession, absolution without personal confession. Cheap grace is grace without discipleship, grace without the cross, grace without Jesus Christ, living and incarnate.[5]

Cheap grace is the merchandise of the false prophet. "Thus you will know them by their fruits." They bring a bogus peace of mind, but no deepening of justice and compassion, no renewal of character, no reformation of society.

No one can be serious about God who is not serious about sin. To be serious about sin is to confess it and repent of it in the presence of a Savior who can bring us through the valley of the shadow of the death of the old self, out into the sunlight of a new kind of life altogether—a life not of duty but of gratitude, filling and overflowing the requirements of moral seriousness.

Delivered from the imprisoning confines of the temple—freed of professionalism, of pigeonholing, and of cheap grace and easy merit, though still aware of their subtle power, we may be ready to hear Jeremiah's temple sermon:

[5] Dietrich Bonhoeffer, *The Cost of Discipleship* (New York: The Macmillan Co., 1959), p. 37.

For if you truly amend your ways and your doings, if you truly execute justice one with another, if you do not oppress the alien, the fatherless or the widow, or shed innocent blood in this place, and if you do not go after other gods to your own hurt, then I will let you dwell in this place, in the land that I gave of old to your fathers for ever (Jer. 7:5-7).

The
Uninspired

Perhaps the most sustained diatribe against false prophets is that found in Jer. 23. From that fiery scripture consider three verses which bear upon our present topic: "Thus says the Lord of hosts: 'Do not listen to the words of the prophets who prophesy to you, filling you with vain hopes; they speak visions of their own minds, not from the mouth of the Lord'" (Jer. 23:16).

> I did not send the prophets,
>   yet they ran;
> I did not speak to them,
>   yet they prophesied (Jer. 23:21).

"I am against the prophets, says the Lord, who steal my words from one another" (Jer. 23:30).

NOT SPEECHLESS

The false prophet is uninspired. This does not mean that he is without words. On the contrary, he may be a very wordy man, even a man cursed by eloquence.

In Sam Spewack's play, *Under the Sycamore Tree,* in which the ants are studying the ways of men, a brilliant scientific ant discovers words. An old conservative among the ants fights the introduction of words into ant society and pleads with the queen to ban them. The queen, feeling otherwise, says, "But I must have words because I might want to say something." The old conservative answers, "What if you have nothing to say?" To this the queen retorts, "Then I shall need more words." [1]

The false prophet may be uninspired, but he is not speechless. It is difficult, in fact, to get him to stop talking long enough to hear his own echo and thus to discover how hollow his words are.

The demand for word production which rolls in upon a prophet, ancient or modern, is a little staggering. Not only is he required to have a weekly sermon—perhaps even two sermons but also there are numerous other occasions and ceremonies for which he is expected to have a word fitly spoken. Much of this speaking is before civic organizations, luncheon clubs, professional schools, colleges, and societies— yes, even lectureships in theological seminaries. Scarcely a committee, class, club, or society of the church attended by the minister adjourns with closing benediction until the minister has been asked to say something; and the minister, out of cowardice or habit, seldom declines, whether he has anything worth saying or not.

If this ceaseless Niagara of words were committed to the printed page it would amount to several books a year—much of it not worth the cost of the paper and ink. But the listening

---

[1] Perry Epler Gresham, *Disciplines of the High Calling* (St. Louis: The Bethany Press, 1954), p. 75.

ear of a prophet's public is enormous and its appetite is voracious. Evidently it is never appeased, let alone satiated. In this fact lies the prophet's temptation. Words are required of him, rivers of words. How is the slow trickle, or the painful drip, of his own thought to fill up this wide riverbed? A young man, contemplating the prospect, is not to be censured too harshly if he feels something akin to panic. Where will he find all these words?

PLAGIARISM

One answer, at least as old as the prophet Jeremiah, is to pirate them from other preachers. Even as early as Jeremiah's day, plagiarism must have been fairly rampant. Else why would Jeremiah have troubled to speak against it? "Behold, I am against the prophets, says the Lord, who steal my words from one another" (Jer. 23:30). The root of the Hebrew word here translated "to steal from" is *ganav* (גנב). When this root is used as a noun it means, bluntly, *a thief*. Plagiarism is, therefore, a species of larceny. A plagiarizing preacher is a reverend robber. And although the concept is logically contradictory and morally repulsive, the practice is alarmingly widespread.

There were periods in the history of the church when the practice of preaching another man's sermons was officially encouraged or even commanded. These were eras in which preaching had died out or fallen into abuse among an ignorant clergy. In an effort to fill up a vacant sermon hour, or to remedy a sick one, various bishops began to publish books of sermons, requiring parish priests to use them. For example, sometime between 822 and 842, at the request of the Archbishop of Mainz, Rabanus Maurus wrote a book of sermons for private reading but especially for use by priests in their pulpits. At the completion of his task the author informed his archbishop, "In obedience to your commands I have composed a book of sermons to be preached to the people on all subjects which I consider necessary for them." [2]

By the fourteenth and fifteenth centuries this practice had grown. One historian reports, "There were books of outlines, collections of various sorts of material, from so-called 'flowers' derived from Scripture and other sources, to fables, tales, illustrations gathered from nature and elsewhere." One book called *Parati Sermones* (prepared sermons) passed through seventeen editions. Perhaps the most amusing of all these books is one published by John Werdena in Amsterdam in 1642. Running through twenty-five editions, it bore the title *Sermones Dormi Secure,* which being interpreted, means, *Sleep Well Sermons.* The title is explained in the author's introduction: "Here happily begin the Sunday Sermons with expositions of the Gospels through the year, quite well known and useful to all priests, pastors, and chaplains, which are also called by the other title Sleep Well, or Sleep without Care, for this reason, that without much study they may be appropriated and preached to the people.[3]

One outline from this book will illustrate Werdena's art. The text is Mark 6:48, "The wind was contrary unto them." There are four points:

1. The east wind blows when a man reflects on the sorrowful condition in which he entered this life. 2. The west wind, when he

[2] Edwin Charles Dargan, *A History of Preaching* (Grand Rapids, Mich., Baker Book House, 1954), I, 168.
[3] *Ibid.,* p. 309.

reflects on bitter death. 3. The south wind, when he thinks of the joys of eternity. 4. The north wind, when he thinks of the terrors of the last judgment.[4]

For at least fifteen years during the reign of Queen Elizabeth I of England, preachers were actually forbidden to preach sermons of their own composition. Instead, they were ordered by royal decree to read homilies from books of sermons provided for the purpose. As late as 1577 Archbishop Grindal protested to the queen that ministers ought to create and deliver their own sermons. For this boldness he was deposed from his office.

King James I began to reverse the trend with his decree that preachers were to deliver a sermon every Sunday, and that at least one of these each month should be his own original composition. But even when official sanction to preach other men's sermons was withdrawn and it came to be expected that a preacher should prepare his own sermons, there were some who favored borrowing. Addison, for example, in *The Spectator*, Number 106, said that he "heartily wished" that more country parsons would stop "wasting their spirits in laborious compositions of their own," and would, instead, preach sermons "penned by great masters." [5]

At any rate, approved or disapproved, the borrowing continued. John Milton in his *Areopagitica*, published in 1644, referred to the "multitude of sermons ready printed and piled up on every text that is not difficult," so that no preacher need ever fear of being in short supply.[6] Harry Major Paull,

---

[4] *Ibid.*, p. 310.
[5] Harry Major Paull, *Literary Ethics* (London: Thornton Butterworth, Ltd., 1928), p. 93.
[6] *Ibid.*, p. 93.

who made a study of pulpit piracy, informs us that "writing sermons for the booksellers was a common task with the Grub Street hacks" in the eighteenth century. Samuel Johnson wrote them at the time when he was living on fivepence a day. In Oliver Goldsmith's *Citizen of the World* the practice is mirrored in the speech of a bookseller's hack, who says, "Would you think it, gentlemen, I have actually written last week sixteen prayers, twelve bawdy jests, and three sermons, all at the rate of sixpence apiece." [7]

One of the most enterprising hucksters of ready-made sermons was a John Trusler, born in 1735. "In 1769, he sent circulars to every parish in England and Ireland proposing to print in script type in imitation of handwriting, about one hundred fifty sermons at the price of one shilling each, in order to save the clergy both study and trouble in transcribing." [8] Needless to say, the scheme was immensely successful, and it is still being imitated.

In his *Commonplace Book* under the heading "An Everyday Advertisement" in 1849, Robert Southey quoted from an advertisement which had appeared forty-two years earlier, in *The Courier* of May 9, 1807. Addressed *Ad Cleros*, it was printed in Latin, presumably so that the laity might not read it. It offered sixty sermons in imitation of handwriting at three pounds (£3). [9]

An article on "The Sermon Trade" appeared in *St. Paul's Magazine*, February, 1869, calling attention to a well-organized commercial enterprise in the hands of about a dozen publishers. This article made an educated guess that twelve hundred

[7] *Ibid.*, p. 94.
[8] Sidney Lee, ed., *National Dictionary of Biography* (London: Smith, Elder & Co., 1899), LVII, 268.
[9] Paull, *Literary Ethics*, p. 96.

75

pirated sermons were then being preached every Sunday in the Church of England. The article quoted the price list of one publisher: A quarter's sermons, fifteen shillings, sixpence; if paid in advance, thirteen shillings, sixpence; a specimen sermon, one shilling, sixpence; a missionary sermon, two shillings, sixpence; sermons for local occasions, ten shillings, sixpence; "visitation sermon," one pound, one shilling. This same advertisement went on to say:

> We are assured that the sermons are composed by "clergymen only of known ability and long parochial experience." The publishers promise in their circulars that especial care will be taken "to prevent their being detected" . . . so "no duplicates are sent to towns," and the purchaser has to promise to preach them in his own parish only; nor may he lend them without the editor's consent.[10]

It would seem that even among pulpit thieves there are rules of honor.

So much for past centuries and for lands across the sea. What about the pulpit of the United States in the twentieth century? So far as I am aware, no comprehensive study has been made, although the data for it are abundant and available. Without going out of my way and without answering a single advertisement or circular, I have over the past eight years accumulated a fat folder of materials which point to a thriving trade in this questionable commodity.

PLAGIARISM IN AMERICA NOW

There is a pulpit service in Missouri offering sermons in quarterly series. The advertising flier says: "Each sermon dupli-

[10] *Ibid.*, p. 97.

cated by offset on 7″ x 8½″ paper (legal size folded). Each sermon complete. Each sermon usable—each sermon has been used! Guaranteed to raise your attendance if used as outlined. 13 sermons plus attendance booster plan only $3.00—published quarterly." Testimonials from satisfied users run like these: "You are helping me to proclaim the Word with Power. My people appreciate my preaching much more now since I have been using your material." "I like them fine. I want others." "These sermons are well worth the $3.00."

I have samples of two monthly magazines, "The Sermon Builder," published in Colorado; and "The Preacher's Sermon Builder," published in Texas. The editor of one of these advertises: "100,000 Preachers Can't Be Wrong." "The intention of Preacher's Sermon Builder is always to suggest a homiletical arrangement of the text. It is never doctrinal. In fact, we strive to keep theology from showing in all of the sermon material we publish. This narrows our purpose down to endeavoring to present a 'gospel message' acceptable to all groups." Then he adds, "We hope every minister will re-work, and re-arrange our suggestive material to suit his own personality and theological beliefs." It is clear, nevertheless, that no rearranging or reworking is necessary. Whole sermons are supplied verbatim. To make transfer to the pulpit smoother, one of these magazines prints its full sermons in typewriter print on pages 11 x 8½ inches, which is standard manuscript size.

There is a *Sermon Outline Quarterly* published in Tennessee. The flier announces that the editor has had "thirty years of experience in the field of sermon outline writing and publishing. A quarter of a million of his sermon outline books has been sold which is evidence of the quality of material you may expect in this new publication." This publishing house also offers a twenty-seven volume set, an *Encyclopedia of Sermon Outlines.*

When it comes to sermon encyclopedias, resources are abundant. Among advertisements that have come to my desk there are three recently published or reprinted. There is *The Biblical Illustrator* from Michigan. It contains fifty-seven volumes arranged chronologically by biblical books. It provides: "Complete sermons, short sermons, sermon outlines, quotations, illustrations, expository notes, practical lessons and anecdotes. . . . Every book of the Bible is included. You simply turn to the text or passage you have chosen, and immediately an overflowing wealth of sermon material comes into view. Most readers report that there is much more material than they can use at one time. This has been carefully chosen from the pulpit masters of yesteryear." Just how far back in "yesteryear" is indicated by such names as Martin Luther, Charles Finney, Henry Ward Beecher, Charles Spurgeon, George Whitefield, and Dwight L. Moody. From these it might seem that the latest word from God arrived sometime in the nineteenth century.

A New York publisher offers *Expository Outlines on the Whole Bible* edited by Charles Simeon, a contemporary of John Wesley. He was born in 1759 and died in 1836. This multivolume work offers no less than "2,536 sermon skeletons." One thinks of the skeletons in the valley of dry bones in the Book of Ezekiel! Specimen pages from this encyclopedia, conveniently annotated, show "clear readable type," "inspiring exhortation," "expository jewels," "forceful illustrations," "lucid explanation," "expository outlines," and "scholarly footnotes." The republishing of this massive work is a costly venture. Clearly, the publishers would not have undertaken it if they did not expect it to sell by the thousands.

Freshly reissued also is James Hastings' *The Great Texts of the Bible* in twenty volumes. Hastings' dates are a little more recent than Charles Simeon's. He lived from 1852 to 1922.

There are other encyclopedias and books of this nature. I am not trying to be comprehensive, merely illustrative. And everything that I have mentioned is now in print, "hot off the griddle." You have but to turn the advertising pages of certain magazines to see still more: "Nine Special Passion Week Sermons. Featuring Seven Words from the Cross. Palm Sunday and Easter Sermons. Three-hole Loose Leaf Book. $2.00 per copy." "The Preacher's Gold Mine." "A Treasury of Sermon Illustrations." "1,001 Sermon Illustrations and Quotations." "440 Snappy Sermon Starters."

At least three firms, getting away from encyclopedias and books, offer ministers' file services, mostly in the area of usable illustrations. One, called "Fingertip Facts," offers sixteen cards a month or 192 cards a year in four categories:

1. Wide World–these facts come on cherry index cards.
2. Background Briefs–these facts come on blue index cards.
3. Church Success–these facts come on yellow index cards.
4. Garden of Gems–these facts come on white index cards.

There is more, much more, but little is to be gained by further enumeration or illustration. It has already become clear that pulpit plagiarism is big business. We cannot even guess how many preachers Sunday by Sunday are preaching these sermons, plucked largely out of the graves of yesterday's masters; but in any reckoning the number has to run into the thousands. It soon becomes plain that we have something here that amounts to a scandal.

While preparing this chapter I received a letter from a new sermon outline service asking me to be one of twenty-five ministers to submit sermons. The letter promised, "A 5% royalty will be paid on each sermon published. While this cannot be known definitely at the moment, the publisher estimates that this should be approximately $100 per sermon." It appears that the business is lucrative to sermon writers as well as to publishers. The letter continues: "Perhaps you can contribute sermons on a regular basis (perhaps four or five a year), but, even if you are not sure now that you would wish to be a regular contributor, we hope that you will submit one sermon to get the service started. Then you can decide whether you wish to continue to participate." Here is a service that proposes to be contemporary; and it confidently expects to find writers who will be lured by flattery and money to cooperate.

Plagiarism is a flagrant violation of preaching, a contradiction in terms. For as Phillips Brooks so aptly said,

Preaching is the communication of truth by man to men. It has in it two essential elements, truth and personality. Neither of these can it spare and still be preaching. . . .

Truth through Personality is our description of real preaching. The truth must come really through the person, not merely over his lips, not merely into his understanding and out through his pen. It must come through his character, his affections, his whole intellectual and moral being. It must come genuinely through him. I think that, granting equal intelligence and study, here is the great difference which we find between two preachers of the Word. The Gospel has come *over* one of them and reaches us tinged and flavored with his superficial characteristics, belittled with his littleness. The Gospel has come *through* the other, and we receive it impressed and winged with all the earnestness and strength that there is in him.[10]

"Therefore, behold, I am against the prophets, says the Lord, who steal my words from one another" (Jer. 23:30).

PLAGIARISM—HARD AND SOFT

It is time for a word about the varieties of plagiarism, for plagiarism may be hard or soft. Hard plagiarism is knowingly pirating another man's sermon word for word while palming it off as one's own. Even here, however, there is room for some variety. Some men may do this habitually, while others may do it occasionally. Some very able men, caught in the rush of a busy week, have been guilty on a few infrequent occasions of appropriating other men's sermons. It would be possible to cite instances. Several years ago a book of sermons by a nationally celebrated American preacher was published posthumously, only to have it discovered that two of the sermons in the book had been plagiarized. This man had a national reputation as a preacher of more than usual originality and brilliance. Nevertheless he was guilty on at least two occasions of pulpit piracy. This was hard plagiarism, but, if we may distinguish degrees of hardness, it was not adamantine.

Similarly, a friend of mine who teaches preaching in another theological seminary published a volume of sermons a few years ago, presented it as a gift to a distinguished American preacher whom he greatly admired, then, several months later,

[10] Phillips Brooks, *Lectures on Preaching* (New York: E. P. Dutton, 1891), pp. 5, 8.

visited the church which that preacher served, only to discover himself listening to one of his own sermons. A surprising and humiliating experience for both men! The explanation which came through the mail a few days later was lame but honest: "I was so hard pressed that I failed to prepare a sermon of my own last week. I read yours and liked it, so I used it." If I were to mention the culprit's name, you would recognize it instantly. This may have been the only breach of pulpit ethics that he ever committed. His ministry was conducted all his life in such a glare of public notice that he could not have done it often. Nevertheless, he did fall into temptation at least once.

One of the most foolhardy instances of plagiarism that I ever heard about happened several years ago. A minister was looking for an associate pastor. Having received a recommendation of one likely candidate, he wrote the young man. Among various questions and requests, he suggested that the candidate might like to submit the manuscript of a sermon. The candidate complied by sending under his own name the full manuscript of one of the minister's own sermons!

This young man did not get the job, but he went on to greater things. He became minister of a metropolitan pulpit where he had a spellbinding career for several years. One Sunday morning, after he had preached a particularly able sermon, he was approached by one of his deacons who had read the sermon a day or two before in a book. Without batting an eye, the accused blithely countered, "But didn't I preach it well, though!" This was truly a case of hard plagiarism.

In soft plagiarism preachers do not appropriate whole sermons. Instead they lift outlines or illustrations from books of illustrations. This might be called piecemeal plagiarism. It is intentional, but it still leaves room for a great deal of a preacher's own work. There are perhaps few men who have not been so captivated by another man's outline that they could hardly resist using it. Some outlines develop a widespread currency in this manner. Perhaps you have heard Charles Reynolds Brown's outline of the Parable of the Good Samaritan. There were in that story, said Brown, three classes of people: (1) Those who said, "What is yours is mine, and I'll take it" (the robbers). (2) Those who said, "What is mine is mine, and I'll keep it" (the priest and Levite). (3) Those who said, "What is mine is yours, and we'll share it" (the Samaritan).

According to the testimony of a personal friend of mine, this sermon originated in considerably less polished form in one of Dean Brown's homiletics classes at Yale Divinity School in 1927. As a teacher of homiletics I have read it more than once in sermons submitted by junior students in beginning preaching classes. But in the early 1950's I heard it used in Lexington, Kentucky, by a bishop of the United Church of South India, who was by now completely unaware of its original author or of the worldwide course it had taken to come to him. I would call that soft plagiarism. Nevertheless, it was one outline that was heard around the world.

Still under soft plagiarism is a kind of pulpit piracy which is unintentional. This is committed by the man whose reading is limited to other men's sermons and to predigested material. He does not know what it is to struggle on his own with great themes, or to read books which require great concentration. When, therefore, he turns to the preparation of sermons he has little choice but to play "Little Sir Echo." He has no sources for anything else. He is not a plagiarist by intention; only by default. Regarding the reading of books Oliver Wendell Holmes once said that a man may milk 300 cows; but he should make his own butter. The trouble with the men we have just been describing is that they do no milking at all; they merely steal pats of butter already churned.

CAUSE AND CURE

When we turn to the cause of plagiarism, hard or soft, we have to consider the views of Jeremiah, who was the first to mention the practice. In the same chapter in which he said, "I am against the prophets . . . who steal my words from one another," he had some things to say that bore on the question:

> I did not send the prophets,
> yet they ran;
> I did not speak to them,
> yet they prophesied (Jer. 23:21).

This picture of prophets on the run without any sure sense of direction is not an inapt description of the busy life of some parish ministers. When one of these is not meeting with a board or a committee, he is dashing to the hospital, or a wedding rehearsal, or riding in a funeral procession to the cemetery. He may be meeting with the Rotary program committee, or the committee on urban renewal, or the mayor's commission on human rights. Somehow he must find time to visit newcomers to the community, to do evangelistic calling and instruct his pre-Easter class in church membership, and to say the invocation or benediction at three or four community functions per week. Hours will be consumed in personal counseling, other hours in planning and conducting services of worship and study. Besides these, he supervises the care and feeding of the addressing machine and the mimeograph, which seem in our time to tyrannize every office and to have such a voracious appetite for paper. The ring of the telephone punctuates his mealtimes and his rare evenings at home with his family. He is, as my colleague, Lewis Smythe has remarked, a man with "residual responsibility." This means that though some other men work from sun to sun a minister's work is never done. He carries a twenty-eight-hour work load on a twenty-four-hour schedule.

Where in the midst of all this is he to find the time to continue the reading and study which were only started by his seminary? When is he to reflect and meditate? When will he prepare his sermons and write an occasional article or book for publication?

It becomes immediately obvious that a minister without a hierarchy of values will go down in the stampede. He will not lead his own life nor guide anybody else's life. He will simply succumb to the pressures and cross-pressures that rush upon him. "I did not send the prophets, yet they ran!"

Jeremiah's cure for this frenzied but uninspired activity is somewhat cryptic:

> But if they had stood in my council,
>   then they would have proclaimed my words to my people,
> and they would have turned them from their evil way,
>   and from the evil of their doings (Jer. 23:22).

In a previous verse in the same twenty-third chapter he has asked,

For who among them has stood in the council of the Lord
to perceive and to hear his word,
or who has given heed to his word and listened? (Jer. 23:18).

The council of the Lord, according to J. Philip Hyatt who
wrote the commentary on Jeremiah for *The Interpreter's Bible,*
was

a council . . . of super-natural beings, presided over by Yahweh.
The lower beings are known variously as "holy ones," "spirits,"
"sons of God," etc.; their existence is no denial of monotheism,
since they were thought of as rendering homage of Yahweh and
under his power. . . . Jeremiah believed that in some manner the
true prophet was actually admitted to such a council where he
received the "word of Yahweh," but that the privilege was denied
to the false prophet.[11]

When one asks the contemporaneous meaning of the council
of the Lord, he may possibly see about three ways of access
to it. The first is to open the book through whose pages we may
keep company with "Gideon, Barak, Samson, Jephthah . . .
David and Samuel and the prophets—who through faith conquered kingdoms, enforced justice, received promises, stopped
the mouths of lions, quenched raging fire, escaped the edge
of the sword, won strength out of weakness, became mighty in
war, put foreign armies to flight" (Heb. 11:32-33). Surely the
council of the Lord will include such worthies as Moses, Isaiah,
Jeremiah, Hosea, and Amos. Their testimony is open to us;
their words are available. Jesus and Luke, Mark, James, and
Paul could not fail to gather with the sons of God in the council of the Almighty. Through the pages of the Bible we may
stand in the midst of their holy company.

[11] *The Interpreter's Bible* (12 vols.; Nashville: Abingdon Press, 1956), V,
992.

This is in keeping with the sound charge to the Timothys of every age:

Remember that from early childhood you have been familiar with the sacred writings which have power to make you wise and lead you to salvation through faith in Christ Jesus. Every inspired scripture has its use for teaching the truth and refuting error, or for reformation of manners and discipline in right living, so that the man who belongs to God may be efficient and equipped for good work of every kind (II Tim. 3:15-17 NEB).

There are many approaches to the reading of the Bible which fall short of its true purpose. The Bible may be read as a museum of literary types or of cultural anthropology. It may be read as an exercise in historical criticism or textual analysis. All these are legitimate objective studies; but all are preliminary. Only when it is read in faith as a book of faith do its pages flame with divine fire, like the burning bush at the foot of Mt. Horeb. Then a divine voice issues from the fire calling us by name.

It has been the experience of thousands that when they will put themselves through the discipline of language and study, and when they will open themselves on the plane of the personal and "come within understanding distance," as Alexander Campbell liked to say, they begin to "hear the sound of a distant drummer." God speaks. I have seen it happen in preaching classes quarter by quarter, year by year. A young man will place himself before a book of the Old or New Testament, study it conscientiously and honestly, then read it as one who is listening. When he comes away from that kind of involvement and begins to tell you what he has heard, you will find him speaking in a new dimension. His words are wiser than he is, winged with a power not his own; and he becomes a servant of the living Word.

We do well to approach the reading of the Bible in private or in public with a prayer like this: "May the bright beams of thy Word, O Lord, pierce every veil that darkens my heart; may thy Word search me, convince, correct and comfort me; through Jesus Christ my Lord."

The second access to the council of God is the life of prayer. To be valid, the life of prayer must be in the name—that is, in the spirit—of Christ. There is a great deal of praying which, at best, is sub-Christian, and at worst is injurious and positively wicked. When I think of some kinds of prayer I am reminded of the recent British invention, the Hovercraft, capable of traveling over sea and land without touching either. It rides on a cushion of air—in the case of prayers, a cushion of hot air. Prayer is more than unctuous "much-speaking," as Jesus said. And it is not pietistic disengagement from the real problems and struggles of daily life. Rather it is standing knee-deep or neck-deep in the muck of life and looking to white clouds sailing across blue skies and seeing God's sun in the heavens. It is taking a celestial bearing upon our human landscape and our human enterprise. It is entering into that kind of honesty with ourselves and with others which we dare not entertain for one instant unless God reigns and his righteousness fills up our inadequacy. It is not a poultice on the symptoms of our malaise; it is the surgical thrust of a scalpel in the hands of the Great Physician, lancing the abscess and letting out the poison.

Moreover, the life of true prayer alternates between alone-ness and togetherness. Unless our life with others—at least a few others—penetrates deeper than politeness so that it becomes a genuine fellowship of mutual concern, minutes or hours spent alone in so-called private devotions will be hollow times of self-flagellation or pious pretense. The Holy Spirit is not sealed in a book; he is abroad among his people, in the depths of their community when it meets in faith and forgiveness, in hope and love. On the other hand, if one is never alone and solitary, there is apt to be little true prayer in his gathering with the congregation.

There is another word about prayer and sermon preparation that ministers should hear. If it is accepted that the sermon in the midst of the congregation is itself an act of worship—a vehicle through which God meets with his people—then it should also be accepted that the right preparation of that sermon is an act of worship. It is as a listener that the minister should prepare to speak; then he will speak as one who is being addressed by the Eternal.

A third access to the council of God is extrabiblical reading and study. A man who studies only one book does not even understand that book. This is because God loves the whole world and works seven days a week, not merely on Sunday. The whole realm of culture and learning is his concern. A man who is sheltered from the yearning, the thoughts, and the hungers of the world is ill-equipped to serve a Master who loved publicans and sinners. In creative literature at its best— that is, in biography, drama, short story, and novels—there "cross the crowded ways of life," and one hears "the cries of race and clan." There he may not learn what God's action may be, but he will come closer to man's need.

Our creative artists are endowed with superior sensitivity. What the inarticulate soul of an age barely whispers, they hear as a shout; what rises in a mist for others, sweeps upon them as a torrential stream. While most of us gaze upon the mask of an age, mistaking it for the real thing, these men who have eyes for the invisible see beneath the mask. They stop asking secondary questions: What shall we eat? What shall we drink? Wherewithal shall we be clothed? They begin asking primary questions which bring us to the verge of time and eternity: Who am I? How do I relate to others? What does my life mean? What is worth living and dying for?

In creative literature of every age the universal themes sound clear. And we begin to hear, as Ralph Waldo Emerson said, not the ticking of the hours and minutes but the tolling of the years and the centuries. We are better prepared to understand and minister to our own time because we are not wholly engulfed by it.

To stand in the council of the Lord we will need at least these three doors of access. Without them we will be not a voice but an echo. The editors of *Fortune* articulated the need clearly: "The ultimate answers to the questions that humanity raises are not, and never have been, in the flesh." Then they go on to say:

The way out is the sound of a voice, not our voice, but a voice coming from something not ourselves, in the existence of which we cannot disbelieve. It is the earthly task of our pastors to hear this voice, to cause us to hear it, and to tell us what it says. . . . Without it we are no more capable of saving the world than we were capable of creating it in the first place.[12]

[12] Editorial from *Fortune* (January, 1940).

REDEEMING THE TIME

The false prophet is, as the title of this chapter indicates, the uninspired. I suspect that he is uninspired because he is undisciplined, not because he intentionally defaults. The key to the problem, then, seems to lie in setting up priorities and "redeeming the time" (Eph. 5:16 ASV). In practical terms this means "chaptering" each month and each week and plotting the course of each day. In our appointment books we have made certain entries—committee meetings, civic clubs, board meetings, wedding rehearsals, and personal conferences. These are our public commitments. What we need is a fuller appointment book which will include not only these public commitments but a number of private appointments to read and study. We need to keep these appointments as conscientiously as we show up for the morning church service and as regularly as we go to meals and to bed. With due allowance for recreation, we should plan our months and weeks in advance. Then we should plot each day early in the morning, establishing the day's priorities. We can do this without being inflexible, without being closed against interruptions.

To keep company with the inspiring is to be inspired, but there must be time for the keeping of such company. If the uninspired are so because they are undisciplined, and if they are undisciplined because they are poor masters of their time, the whole problem boils down to a single issue. A missionary once put it this way: Reflecting upon the almost superhuman demands made upon a minister in a foreign land, he said, "A missionary has to learn how to distribute his neglect." This means sorting out the trivial from the important, the mechanical and impersonal from the personal. It means less counting of paper clips and turning of the mimeograph machine and more pastoral work. It also means more time for mental and spiritual renewal.

When we fail to do this, we lamely excuse ourselves by saying, "I could not find the time." We act as though Socrates and Plato, Jesus and Paul, Augustine and Aquinas, Luther and Calvin, Barth and Tillich had more hours in a day than we do. Each man's day is twenty-four hours long, no less but no more. Given differences in talent—which are not as diverse as we like to think—the great difference between the wastrel and the worker is that the wastrel is waiting to find the time while the worker is redeeming it. Time is the metal from which we mint the coin of creative living; waste this wealth and we end as spiritual paupers.

Living
Behind
a Mask

The most caustic words of Jesus did not *fall* from his lips; they were shot like arrows from a bow. Their target was the Pharisees, in many ways the most disciplined, the most conscientious, and the most rational people of their day. Jesus called them *hypocrites,* not once but many times. On his lips the word was a stinging epithet.

Hypocrite, a Greek word of noble meaning, came down in the world and fell into evil company. Quite literally it means "one who answers." Originally, as William Barclay reminds us, it referred to several public figures—to an interpreter of oracles and dreams, to an orator like Demosthenes, to a reciter of poetry. Eventually it came to mean an actor on a stage, a man who played a part. Thus in ancient Greek society the emotional color of the word *hypocrites* was entirely favorable. It referred to honored men in approved professions. But by the time the word appeared in the Septuagint Old Testament it was colored with disapproval. This came from the association of the word with a dramatic actor. It took the actor, the *hypocrite,* from his stage and cast him in the midst of life as a man who was never himself, a man who was always acting out a role, playing a part.

On the face of it, Jesus' application of this epithet to the Pharisees is startling. It does not appear that the Pharisees were spiritual confidence men playing upon the credulity of the people. They were not consciously fraudulent. They were, as we have said, the most disciplined, the most conscientious, the most rational people of their day. If they were hypocrites, they were unconscious of their hypocrisy. If they were acting a part, they were so accustomed to the role that they had confused their personage with their person.

From this it would appear that there is such a thing as unconscious hypocrisy and that it may afflict not the derelicts of society but its moral and spiritual leaders. So subtle and so pervasive is the temptation to hypocrisy that Jesus thought it wise to warn his disciples against it: "Beware of the leaven of the Pharisees" (Matt. 16: 6, 11-12). This is a disturbing realization. It means that Pharisaism may not have died with the passing of the Pharisees of Judaism in the first century A.D. It means that there may be such a thing as Pharisaism in Christendom. It means that you and I, the most disciplined, the most conscientious, the most rational people of our day, may be Pharisees, men acting a part.

THEATRICAL GOODNESS

One charge which Jesus lodged against the Pharisees was their love of the limelight. "They do all their deeds to be seen by men; for they make their phylacteries broad and their fringes long, and they love the place of honor at feasts and the best seats in the synagogues, and salutations in the market places, and being called rabbi by men" (Matt. 23:5-7). Jesus warned his disciples against this addiction to publicity: "Beware of practicing your piety before men in order to be seen by them" (Matt. 6:1). And he saw the love of popularity as one of the most threatening evils his disciples would face: "Woe to you, when all men speak well of you, for so their fathers did to the false prophets" (Luke 6:26).

It is easy to exempt oneself from such warnings. Because we do not wear long robes with tassels, because we do not bind phylacteries on our arms and foreheads, we may feel that these warnings refer to another day. Perhaps it cannot be as easily denied that we "love the place of honor at feasts." As ministers, we usually sit at the head table, even if we have no other function than to give the invocation. We also usually get the best seats in all religious assemblies—if not on the platform, then someplace only slightly less prominent.

For a number of years I was pastor to a church in a college town. Seldom did a Sunday pass without visitors in the congregation, sometimes even visiting clergymen. One Sunday morning as I met with the choir for the prayer before the beginning of the service, an usher brought me a note, informing me that the Reverend Mr. Blank was in the congregation. Mr. Blank himself had sent the announcement. Why? Obviously so that he would have a chief seat in the synagogue— an invitation to the chancel, perhaps; a request to read the scripture, make the pastoral prayer, or even preach the sermon; at the very least a nice public notice to the effect that the Reverend Mr. Blank, distinguished minister of Such-and-Such Church, was present and we were highly honored to have him in our midst. Here was a man so accustomed to the limelight that the thought of worshiping like any other member of the congregation was intolerable to him. He simply had to seize upon the occasion and squeeze the juice of personal publicity out of it.

While you are gathering stones to cast at this man, and before you cast any, recall your own pleasure at being recognized when you attended a church in a neighboring city at vacation time. Yes, most of us "love the place of honor . . . the best seats in the synagogues, and salutations in the market places." And while we do not relish being called "Rabbi," may not be deeply warmed by "Reverend," and may be positively repulsed by "Brother," we are visibly pleased if someone, accurately or not, takes the trouble to address us as "Doctor."

Several years ago, before I had received an honorary doctorate, I had a speaking engagement for a Sunday evening union service in a certain American city. While we were waiting in the pastor's study for the hour of service, the pastor handed me the printed program. I glanced at it and discovered that he had wrongly credited me with a doctor's degree. I tried to set him straight, but he stopped me. "That's all right. I don't have a doctor's degree either; but you'll notice that one is listed after my name, too. The men in this town who have honorary doctor's degrees are no better preachers than you and I are, so I gave doctor's degrees to both of us."

The craving for publicity can become an addiction. We can be "hooked" on it as some men are hooked on narcotics. Why is this so? Of course, all men want the approval of their fellows; all men crave public recognition. In this craving, ministers are like everybody else—only more so. Perhaps we had better admit—once daily—that one of the attractions of the ministry for us, like the attraction of moth to the flaming candle, was the spotlight of public recognition that the profession so obviously offered us.

The situation of a Protestant minister in America is so arranged as to accentuate this appeal. One vacation Sunday some years ago I attended Mass in a Roman Catholic cathedral. At the conclusion of the ceremony, the priest turned to address certain announcements to the congregation. One announcement was a stinging rebuke, a reprimand such as only an angry parent considerably provoked might administer to naughty children. As I listened to the priest's searing words, I found myself thinking, "A thing like this could not happen in a Protestant church; any minister who dared to do it would find himself unemployed the next morning." Priests, you see, are appointed by their bishops; they are not elected through popular vote by the congregation. However, if the priest's freedom from democratic control may tend to increase his natural arrogance, the Protestant minister's dependence upon the support of the people may tend to bring out other vices.

The "successful" Protestant minister has to acquire certain skills of wooing public favor. To begin with, he has to have a personality magnetic enough to win the majority of a congregation to support him. And although it is too much to expect that he will please all the people all the time, it is positively necessary for him to please most of the people most of the time, if he is to continue as their minister.

Under such pressure what minister is not tempted to win his way by flattery, by unfailing amiability, through an inexhaustible store of funny stories, and by submerging his role as a prophet? Several years ago the American Council on

Education developed an inventory of "General Goals of Life." which has aimed at testing the life philosophies of college students. It was based upon choices among twenty general goals such as "Doing my duty"; "Serving the community"; "Momentary pleasures"; "Mild, but lasting pleasures—happiness"; "Adventure—daring new experiences"; "Security"; and "Survival—continued existence." One student put this last goal at the head of his list: "If you don't survive you can't do anything else." In much the same manner a minister might rationalize putting popularity at the head of the list: "If you aren't popular, you can't keep your church, or lead the people anywhere."

Nevertheless, the consequences may be devastating. Among several possible consequences, consider four:

First, there is *the well-known ministerial manner*. This is the sort of thing for which the stoic philosopher reprimanded a disciple when he asked him, "Why do you walk around looking as though you had swallowed an obelisk?"

In 1824, through his magazine *The Christian Baptist,* Alexander Campbell was training some of his best artillery on young preachers. He noted with regret the "ministerialization" of a young theological student who "gradually assumes a sanctimonious air":

A holy gloom overspreads his face, and a pious sedateness reigns from his eyebrows to his chin. . . . His words flow on with a solemn slowness, and every period ends with a heavenly cadence. There is a kind of angelic demeanor in his gait, and a seraphic sweetness in all his movements. With his sunday coat on a sabbath morn, he puts on a mantle of deeper sanctity, and imperceptibly learns the three grand tones—the sabbath tone, the pulpit tone, and the praying tone—these are the devout, the more devout and the most devout.[1]

There is no need to belabor the point. Ministerial tone is a fairly common affliction of men in the pulpit. And as for ministerial manner, who needs a description? A somewhat uninhibited friend of mine, after a service of installation with several ministers on the platform, once said to me with an impish gleam in his eye, "I always like to watch ministers singing a hymn!" Could it be that he was thinking, "Sing, choirs of angels, sing in exultation"?

A second devastating consequence of popularity-mindedness is *the danger that we will come to believe the flattery we encourage.* The poet Vachel Lindsay, overwhelmed by publicity and adulation just after the publication of his *Collected Poems,* wrote a friend:

I need a Handy Guide to Privacy, to serenity, to meditation, to delicacy of fancy, to village quietness, to secret prayer. . . . My manager . . . is determined to national-tour me again, Bryanize me if possible. My two publishers back the idea, and I am sure of flattery and fried chicken in every town, while slowly disintegrating.[2]

A third consequence is *word-of-mouth merit.* Week by week we say a great number of noble things. In such a situation it is easy to mistake the saying of the truth for the doing of the truth. Thomas Carlyle said, "It is a sad but sure truth that every time you speak of a fine purpose, especially if with eloquence and to the admiration of bystanders, there is the less

[1] Alexander Campbell, "The Clergy, No. IV," *The Christian Baptist* (January 5, 1824).
[2] C. P. Lee, "Adulation and the Artist," *Saturday Review* (August 10, 1940), p. 18.

chance of your ever making a fact of it in your own poor life."

A fourth devastating consequence of popularity-mindedness is *the loss of identity, the shattering of clear ministerial mission.* If the goal is to please all of the people most of the time, or most of the people all the time, our ministry becomes a form of St. Vitus' dance, which Kyle Haselden has characterized as "external spasms and twitchings but no central control." Haselden goes on to say,

> In far more cases than would admit it, the minister is overburdened because he wants to be overburdened. He wears many hats in church and community because the multiple roles they represent constitute his only identity, his image of himself. This man's name is Legion; his sense of integrity is dependent not upon his being one thing but precisely upon his being many things. His ministry is a "shish kebab" and the more items of activity and responsibility he can add to his skewer, the less he worries about the absence of the main course.[3]

Turning from the disaster to the prevention or the cure, what is there to say? Perhaps we could begin by renouncing the heresy that the voice of the people is the voice of God. We might go on to outgrow the little boy antics and the piping imperative, "Look at me! Look at me!" Then, we might even grow up to the maturity of the disciple Philip, who understood the real yearning of people in the request of the Greeks who came seeking the Master: "Sir, we would see Jesus."

MORALISTIC GOODNESS

Closely allied with the theatrical goodness which hungers for applause and popularity is moralistic goodness. It grows out of

[3] Haselden, *The Urgency of Preaching*, p. 110.

a kind of moral earnestness in many ways vigorous and admirable. Paul drew a picture of such a man—a self-portrait—in his Philippian letter: "Of the people of Israel, of the tribe of Benjamin, a Hebrew born of Hebrews, as to the law a Pharisee, as to zeal a persecutor of the church, as to righteousness under the law blameless" (Phil. 3:5-6), but still a man without love and peace.

According to Luke, Jesus told his famous parable of the Pharisee and the publican "to some who trusted in themselves that they were righteous and despised others" (Luke 18:9). Here, in these few words, we have the two main characteristics of moralistic goodness—self-justification and judgment of others. They go together; in fact, they are the two sides of the same attitude. To justify oneself, one must despise others. He must measure himself against others to their disadvantage.

Self-justification—the Apostle Paul wrote from his own experience when he addressed himself to that topic. Notice how contemporary he becomes and how uncomfortably close to us he comes when we paraphrase Rom. 9:30–10:4, changing *Jews* to *ministers* and *Gentiles* to *laymen:*

What shall we say then? Uneducated laymen who never studied in a seminary are often more Christian than men who have graduated and have been hooded with a Bachelor of Divinity degree. Why is this? Because laymen are not trying to prove how righteous they are. They come to God in faith and bring nothing but a deep sense of their need. Ministers, on the other hand, come to God with their hands full of the good deeds they have been doing and with their heads full of determination to be as good as they are expected to be. They stub their toes and stumble over their own goodness, and by just that much they fall short of the goodness that God would give them, if they would only stop trying to be paragons of virtue.

101

Brethren, my heart's desire and prayer to God for ministers is that they too may be saved. I know from experience that they spend much time with religion, but they are not always religious. They often go about trying to prove to others—and to themselves—how righteous they are; and so they are not open to the righteousness that can come only from God. To be blunt about it, they are not looking for a Savior. They think they can still save themselves. They know God only as lawgiver and judge; they do not yet know him as redeemer. Actually, in spite of the fact that they call themselves Christians, they are living under the law, when they could be living as forgiven and liberated men under the grace of Christ.

I, for one, believe that it is natural for a young Christian minister to begin on the plane of self-justification. He approaches his lifework with moral seriousness. He knows that God does not condone evil. That is to say, he has met God as lawgiver and judge. But he stands before the bar of divine judgment as one accused—accused by his own conscience; and he stands there as one suing for acquittal. He has not yet met God as redeemer. He has no other recourse at this stage than to try to win God's approval by his own moral achievement. He is compelled by the seriousness of his predicament to try to justify himself.

Years ago I was intimately acquainted with a high school youth who had two close friends, one preparing to enter medicine, the other, law. He himself was planning to be a Christian minister. The three friends were on good terms; they studied together and played together. One day the budding lawyer shot the budding minister a question: "What makes you think you are good enough to be a minister?" It was a casual question; in the mind of the questioner it probably had little importance. But to the mind of the questioned it could not have been more cruel if it were a red-hot branding iron. He could

102

not reply; but he spent the next several years trying to answer that question, for it was also his own question. At every stage of his life he found himself saying, "I know that I am not good enough—yet." Then, firming up his willpower and gritting his moral teeth, he would say, "But I will make myself good enough; I will become worthy of God's approval." In those years he was puritanical and judgmental toward other people, but he was not half as harsh with them as he was with himself. In those early years he was caught in Paul's dilemma, though he did not connect it with Paul's words: "I can will what is right, but I cannot do it. For I do not do the good I want, but the evil I do not want is what I do" (Rom. 7:18b-19).

The feeling he experienced in those years was one of almost utter loneliness. It was the loneliness of a solitary person standing before the unapproachable light of the living God. He did not know it then, but he has since discovered that this is the situation of the vast majority of young men entering the Christian ministry. Most of them labor under the lash of their own judgment, striving for self-justification. They are all stung with the question, "What makes you think you are good enough to be a Christian minister?" And they are determined to make themselves worthy by the exercise of their own goodness.

This fact does not always appear in outward behavior, for there are times when such a young man may appear, in his own language, to be "goofing off." As a matter of fact, he alternates between feverish striving after perfection and compulsive loafing; between the exaltation of fine achievement and the despair of ever doing anything that halfway measures up to his own ideals. He lives under the lash of the cruel ques-

103

tion, "What makes you think you are good enough to be a minister?"

The goodness that a man can achieve under such circumstances is at best negative. It is like Samuel's address to the people after the coronation of Saul: "Here I am; testify against me before the Lord and before his anointed. Whose ox have I taken? Or whose ass have I taken? Or whom have I defrauded? Whom have I oppressed? Or from whose hand have I taken a bribe to blind my eyes with it?" (I Sam. 12:3). The answer was clear; Samuel had not robbed anybody; he had not enslaved anybody; and he had taken no bribes. Most of us could say the same. Nevertheless, it is not good enough; it is negative. Those who have visited the religious shrines at Kyoto or Nara, Japan, will remember seeing the carvings of the three monkeys which have been reproduced and sold widely as souvenirs. One monkey holds his hands over his eyes, a second covers his ears, and a third, his mouth: "See no evil, hear no evil, speak no evil." It is a perfect symbol of self-justification and negative goodness. It is not good enough. For monkeys it may suffice, but it will always fail for human beings. In relation to ourselves, moralistic goodness makes monkeys of us.

In relation to others, self-justification changes us into snarling cats. The reason for this is simple. Self-salvation through moralistic goodness is an attempt at self-justification which cannot even half succeed without the mechanisms of projection, rationalization, and blame. Self-justification and the harsh judgment of others go together; they are two sides of the same thing.

Someone will object that the harsh judgment of others is inconsistent with the pharisaic goal of popularity, discussed in the first part of this chapter. The answer is that theatrical goodness and contempt for people are entirely homogeneous. The performer needs people, but he need not love them or even like them. He needs them as an audience for his own stellar performance; he needs their applause. He needs people in order to sway them, to give him a sense of power. But he need have no love for them. He need develop no compassionate concern for them. Indeed, insofar as a minister is motivated by such an attitude, he will despise others. He will despise them for the simple reason that they are not quick enough or loud enough in their applause and flattery; or, more usually, because they are slow to implement his programs. In particular, there will be obstreperous elders and negative deacons who will receive a double portion of his wrath. In such a state he will be primed for the mental act of ministerial murder. What minister, in anger, has never said, "What this church needs is a dozen well-placed funerals"?

Thus the false prophet appears as God's angry man. He becomes the voice of wrath in the midst of the congregation. He castigates and punishes his people under the hallowing banner of righteous indignation. He is a man at war, not with Satan and his hosts, but with flesh and blood, with human enemies.

The amazing thing is that people will put up with this, and even welcome it. Why this approval of pulpit pugilism? There are good reasons. For one thing, a great many people feel guilty. They want to be punished so they will be at peace again with an inflamed conscience, but they do not want to be punished too severely. A tongue-lashing from an authorized preacher seems to fill the bill exactly. It is a fine way of paying for sin without repenting of it. The tongue is a lash that does not draw blood. One layman put it this way, "When I go out the church door after a sermon I want to feel like a dirty dog!"

John Steinbeck has given this theme classic treatment in his recent autobiographical *Travels With Charley in Search of America*. He describes his reaction to an old-fashioned fire and brimstone sermon he heard in Vermont:

He [the preacher] spoke of hell as an expert, not the mush-mush hell of these soft days, but a well-stoked, white-hot hell served by technicians of the first order. This reverend brought it to a point where we could understand it, a good hard coal fire, plenty of draft, and a squad of open-hearth devils who put their hearts into their work, and their work was me. I began to feel good all over. For some years now God has been a pal to us, practicing to-getherness, and that causes the same emptiness a father does playing softball with his son. But this Vermont God cared enough about me to go to a lot of trouble kicking the hell out of me. He put my sins in a new perspective. Whereas they had been small and mean and nasty and best forgotten, this minister gave them some size and bloom and dignity. I hadn't been thinking very well of myself for some years, but if my sins had this dimension there was some pride left. I wasn't a naughty child but a first rate sinner, and I was going to catch it.

I felt so revived in spirit that I put five dollars in the plate, and afterward, in front of the church, shook hands warmly with the minister and as many of the congregation as I could. It gave me a lovely sense of evil-doing that lasted clear through till Tuesday.[4]

It is clear that there is a kind of satisfaction to those who take their medicine under such punitive preaching. It pro-

[4] John Steinbeck, *Travels with Charley in Search of America* (New York: The Viking Press, 1962), p. 71.

vides a substitute absolution difficult to distinguish from the real thing.

But there is something more. It also provides a channel for pent-up resentments and hostilities. Most of the time people simply refuse to be the target; they join the preacher with some glee and help him in blasting their enemies. Henry Ward Beecher once said that the church was filled with baldheaded sinners who got that way when the message of the gospel passed over their heads, hitting the people in the row behind them. The characteristic remark of a parishioner as he shakes hands with the preacher after such a sermon is, "Well, Reverend, you certainly gave it to them this morning!" And the preacher, all smiles outwardly, inwardly groans because his real target is now shaking hands with him, feeling more self-righteous than ever.

This is the tried and tested formula of demagogues—to build up people's self-esteem by sanctioning and channeling their resentments. Beneath the placid, civilized exteriors of modern men, deep in the unconscious or subconscious basement of the mind, fires of resentment and hatred lie like molten lava in the subterranean caverns of a volcano. Texans despise Mexicans; Californians resent Nipponese; New Englanders hate Jews; and the whole country smolders against Negroes. Japanese hate Koreans; Arabs hate Israelis; Algerians hate the French; Red Chinese hate Red Russia; we hate both. Tenants hate landlords. Daughters-in-law hate mothers-in-law. Labor hates management. Management hates government.

Contrary to the lyrics of one song from the play *South Pacific*, men do not have to be taught to hate. They do it naturally, and with venom. The man who knows that most people are afraid and frustrated and that fear and frustration

107

breed anger; who then will nurse that anger, praise it as patriotism and righteous indignation, kindle it into a flame— that man, in this age of anxiety and frustration, will have a following. Adolf Hitler and Joseph McCarthy, Robert Welch, and Malcolm X have proved this. The mind of modern man is in a murderous and hysterical condition. The false prophet, himself deeply resentful, both nurtures the mass hysteria and rides to power upon it.

Does this mean that there is no legitimate indignation against social injustices? That a true prophet must never be angry? A brief glimpse of Jesus and the prophets will answer that question. But the characteristic standpoint of the true prophet who is as "a fortified city, an iron pillar, and bronze walls, against the whole land" (Jer. 1:18), is even more profoundly *with* his people. His consternation is born of his compassion:

> O that my head were waters,
>   and my eyes a fountain of tears,
> that I might weep day and night
>   for the slain of the daughter of my people!
>   (Jer. 9:1).

In the same mood the greatest of the prophets, six hundred years later, wept over Jerusalem (Luke 19:41-44). God does engage in controversy with his people. The true prophet must be the voice of God's almighty "nay" in a corrupt and evil time, but he is engaged in something holier than self-justification and social punishment.

Moralistic goodness, if it masquerades as Christian, is false prophecy. Nevertheless, it may be a necessary preparation for true prophecy. That is to say, although moralism cannot double for Christianity, it can prepare us for Christianity. For moralism is our preliminary, though imperfect, apprehension of the moral seriousness that makes life significant. It is our experience of the law, which, to use the Phillips translation, was "like a strict governess in charge of us until we went to the school of Christ and learned to be justified by faith in him" (Gal. 3:24). The Greek word which Phillips here translated *strict governess* and which the Revised Standard Version renders *custodian*, is *paidagogos* (παιδαγωγός). It referred to a special kind of servant among wealthy Greeks and Romans, a trustworthy slave who was charged with the duty of supervising the life and morals of boys. A boy was not allowed to step out of the house until the age of manhood unless accompanied by his *paidagogos*. The moral law is our *paidagogos* who brings us to Christ. There, in the school of the Master Teacher, we will learn of the righteousness of God which is expressed in costly love and grace, and of the justification by grace through faith which brings all self-justification to an end.

Wheat and Tares
Growing
Together

Here is another parable that he put before them: "The kingdom of Heaven is like this. A man sowed his field with good seed; but while everyone was asleep his enemy came, sowed darnel among the wheat, and made off. When the corn [wheat] sprouted and began to fill out, the darnel could be seen among it. The farmer's men went to their master and said, 'Sir, was it not good seed that you sowed in your field? Then where has the darnel come from?' 'This is an enemy's doing,' he replied. 'Well then,' they said, 'shall we go and gather the darnel?' 'No,' he answered; 'in gathering it you might pull up the wheat at the same time. Let them both grow together till harvest; and at harvest-time I will tell the reapers, "Gather the darnel first, and tie it in bundles for burning; then collect the wheat into my barn"' (Matt. 13:24-30 NEB)

What shall we do with the false prophet and with the heretic? In the parable of the tares in the wheat field we have a strong directive from the Master Teacher. Fraudulence among the faithful; antichrist among Christians, is represented here by an alien sowing. The Greek word is *zizánia* (ζιζάνια) The King James Version translates this *tares;* the Revised Standard Version simply calls it *weeds;* but the New English Bible becomes quite specific, for there it is *darnel.* The scientific name is *lolium temulentum.* The Jews called it, in Hebrew, *zunim* (זונים) which seems to mean *bastard wheat.* The point of the parable is closely tied up with the fact that the alien sowing is not just any kind of weed but a particular kind, a bastard wheat, so similar in appearance to the genuine plant that even a skilled farmer cannot detect the difference until the grain heads out. But by that time the roots of the darnel are so intertwined with the roots of the wheat that an uprooting of the alien intruder would destroy the wheat harvest. Also closely tied into the point of the parable is the fact that the grain of the darnel is poisonous, that eating it produces dizziness and sickness. Such poisonous grain must be separated from the wheat before it is ground into flour and eaten as bread, but the separation cannot take place until harvesttime.

We would perhaps need to search a long time to find a more apt symbol for false prophecy than that of the darnel sowed by an enemy in a good wheat field. The false prophet is nearly impossible to distinguish from the true. His life is so closely intertwined with the life of true believers that every human effort to root him out works great wrong upon the faithful. Nonetheless, the false prophet is there in God's field by the hand of the Adversary. His teaching is not bread. It should be marked by a skull and crossbones, for it is poison. In our handling of false prophecy we can be instructed by this parable.

111

NO WHEAT WITHOUT TARES

First, let us notice that the tares are Satan's sowing, and that they are planted, not in their own plot, but in the midst of the wheat.

There is little need to develop this point here; it has already received rather full treatment in the first chapter. We are simply pointing to the fact that the "abomination of desolation" appears, not in the brothel, but in the temple. Satan disguises himself as an angel of light and false religion appears as a counterfeit currency. It succeeds only by being mixed with and mistaken for sound currency.

One further aspect of the matter should not escape us, however; this is the simple fact that no wheat field is without tares. No religion is free of diabolical impurities.

This mixture of the false and the true was brought home to me afresh several months ago when I was rereading a diary by Bernal Díaz del Castillo, one of the five hundred conquistadors under Cortés who conquered Mexico between 1517 and 1521. Human sacrifice at the pyramids of the sun scandalized the Spanish Christians. Of these Díaz wrote:

> Every day we saw sacrificed before us three, four or five Indians whose hearts were offered to the idols and their blood plastered on the walls, and the feet arms and legs of the victims were cut off and eaten, just as in our country we eat beef brought from the butchers. I even believe that they sell it by retail in the . . . markets.

Then Díaz described eight of the Aztec priests:

> These priests wore black cloaks like cassocks and long gowns reaching to their feet, and some had hoods like those worn by

112

canons, and others had smaller hoods like those worn by Dominicans, and they wore their hair very long, down to the waist, with some even reaching down to the feet, covered with blood and so matted together that it could not be separated, and their ears were cut to pieces by way of sacrifice, and they stank like sulphur, and they had another bad smell like carrion.

With so much that was false was there anything at all that was good about this Aztec religion? After such exposure to its horror, we are hardly prepared for what Díaz says next: "[It was said], and we learned that it was true, these priests were the sons of chiefs and they abstained from women, and they fasted on certain days, and what I saw them eat was the pith of seeds of cotton when the cotton was being cleaned." [1]

Here we meet with the rigors of self-denial and self-control associated with Christian monasticism—chastity (even celibacy), fasting, and a limited vegetarian diet. This is not uncontrolled bestiality; it is self-abnegating, self-transcending service to a god whose majesty burns with the fierceness of the noonday sun in the tropics. This is Abraham on Mount Moriah offering his son Isaac—but hearing no restraining voice and seeing no ram with horns caught in the thicket. Here on the pyramids of the sun we come upon mystery and terror of ultimate concerns and loyalties that bless and burn with devilish fury and supernal brilliance. The wheat and the tares grow together in the same field. There are tares, but the wheat is there also.

The same mixture of the godly and the diabolical is seen in what Cortés did after destroying the Aztec idols:

[1] Bernal Díaz del Castillo, *The Discovery and Conquest of Mexico, 1517-1521*, trans. A. P. Maudslay (New York: Farrar, Straus and Cudahy, 1956), pp. 102, 104, 105.

113

Then he ordered all the Indian masons in the town to bring plenty of lime so as to clean the place and clear away the blood which encrusted the cues and to clean them thoroughly. The next day when they were whitewashed, an altar was set up, and he told the people to adorn the altar with garlands and always keep the place swept and clean. He then ordered four of the priests to have their hair shorn, and to change their garments and clothe themselves in white, and always keep themselves clean, and he placed them in charge of the altar and of that sacred image of Our Lady. So that it should be well looked after, he left there as hermit one of our soldiers named Juan de Torres de Córdoba, who was old and lame. He ordered our carpenters to make a cross and place it on a stone support which we had already built and plastered over.[2]

One does not have much confidence that these "instant-Christians," baptized at the point of the sword and with little more preparation than a lay sermon, a bath, a haircut, and a change of robes, would successfully negotiate the passage out of paganism into an unpaganized Christianity. Surely the resultant church would have to be a wheat field in which the tares were already flourishing. But such is the church, in varying degree, in every land and culture. It is a wheat field—God's wheat field—but the Adversary has sowed tares in it. No wheat field is without its tares. No religion is without the voice of the false prophet in the sanctuary.

What, then, is to be done? I suspect that the majority of us are like the farmer's men who wanted to root out the tares.

THE URGE TO UPROOT THE TARES

In fact, history has shown that *those entrusted with the cultivation of God's acre have an almost uncontrollable urge to rush*

[2] *Ibid.,* p. 105.

into the field and begin the uprooting of every noxious plant.
This is nothing other than a fervent attempt to achieve a pure
church in which there are no sinners.

This uprooting of the tares takes various forms. On the one
hand, there are the direct attacks of heresy trials, witch hunts,
and inquisitions. These are violent uprooting operations. On
the other hand, there are the disengagements of monastic withdrawal and of sectarian separatism. Less violent but no more
successful, these are attempts to plant a wheat field in a
choice plot and then to fence it high and impregnable against
the enemy who tries to invade and sow the tares.

The violent uprooting of the tares has given us some of
the bloodiest chapters in the history of intolerance. The lyrical
"faith chapter" in the Letter to the Hebrews preserves an
ancient catalogue of such violent uprootings in Old Testament
days:

Some were tortured, refusing to accept release. . . . Others suffered
mocking and scourging, and even chains and imprisonment. They
were stoned, they were sawn in two, they were killed with the
sword; they went about in skins of sheep and goats, destitute,
afflicted, ill-treated . . . wandering over deserts and mountains,
and in dens and caves of the earth (Heb. 11:35b-38).

In her novel *Cities of the Flesh* Zoé Oldenbourg has written
vividly of the church's attempt to stamp out the Albigensian
heresy in southern France early in the thirteenth century.
Crusaders brought heretical cities under armed assault,
breached the walls, sacked the ruins for booty, and subjected
women and children to rapine, to fire, and slaughter. This was
the work not of lawless hoodlums but of Christian knights with
crosses emblazoned on their shields. They went forth in

response to the call of the pope, and they marched to the battle cry, "God wills it!" Celibate Dominican monks administered the inquisition. Their victims were semiascetic, self-denying Christians admittedly more impervious to luxury and to bribery than most of the orthodox clergy. They were men of incorruptible honesty and of unexampled charity toward the poor. What then was their crime? They were guilty of a mistaken theology; their beliefs were in error. For these errors they were grilled for hours by menacing tribunals. They were examined under torture of whip, thumbscrew, and the rack, or thrown into black dungeons to rot for weeks and months until their bodies wasted away to bags of bones and their reason fled. Then before solemn congregations assembled at the Mass they were given one last chance to recant. Refusing that they were herded, still in chains, to the open plazas, where, after the pomp and circumstance of solemn religious processions, the stakes piled high with faggots waited to receive them as human torches. Not content with burning the living, the zealous friars exhumed the corpses of other heretics and, impervious to the stench, carted the putrefying bodies to the plazas and hurled them into the flames.

Those who recanted were treated more mercifully. They were allowed to go to confession and to receive communion. Then, with no treasure but the grace of God and the knowledge that they had saved their immortal souls from the flames of hell, their property and wealth confiscated, and, dressed in chains, they were made to do penance by spending the rest of their lives in prison.

The history of religion is full of this sort of thing. Protestantism is not free of it. Luther A. Weigle reports,

From the fourteenth century to the eighteenth Europe was cursed with the witchcraft delusion. The theory, first definitely formulated by the University of Paris, was that the witch had renounced her baptism and taken Satan for her God, surrendering herself to him, body and soul, to be used as the instrument of his evil purposes. She had thus become the enemy of her fellow creatures, and should be hunted out and destroyed as one would destroy the seeds of a deadly pestilence. All over Europe the witch fires were fed.[3]

The fever crossed the Atlantic, and, between February 1692 and January 1693, twenty-two convicted witches were hung in Salem, Massachusetts, under the New England Protestant theocracy.

Christianity in the twentieth century has burned no witches, but it has conducted its heresy trials, pronounced its anathemas, and exercised its excommunications. The fire of such intolerance even gave us a good singeing at Lexington Theological Seminary in 1917 when one faculty member accused his colleagues of heresy and sought to have them dismissed. The fervent attempt of pious men to uproot the tares from the Lord's wheat field has been going forward through the centuries.

Concurrent with this more violent method of dealing with the tares, a less violent method has prevailed through the ages. This has been the attempt to plant a wheat field of pure grain in a choice plot and then to fence it securely against those who would sow tares. This refers to the disengagements of monastic withdrawal and sectarian separation. We are well acquainted with monasticism in its Roman and Eastern forms,

[3] Luther A. Weigle, *American Idealism* ("Pageant of America Series," vol. X [New Haven: Yale University Press, 1928]), p. 53.

but we may be less aware of its Protestant forms in the new world. At South Elkhorn, six miles from Lexington, there is the meetinghouse of "the traveling church," a congregation which migrated out of Virginia into the bluegrass region of Kentucky through the Cumberland Gap in 1792. The whole congregation migrated in a body, as a religious colony, with high utopian hopes. This was not an isolated event in pioneer America. Recall also the solidly built Shaker towns that dot the map of the eastern United States. One of these stands only eighteen miles south of Lexington—a visible witness to a Protestant millenarianism which took shape more than a century and a half ago.

At least one of the causes for denominationalism was the desire to purify the church. Disciples of Christ, for example, developed on the American frontier in the spirit of a new start in a new world and with the hope of leaving behind the errors of Christendom which had developed since the apostolic age. It was no accident that Alexander Campbell's crusading periodical (issued from 1830 to 1870) was named *The Millennial Harbinger*. In the end it has developed that the dream of "restoring the ancient order and the ancient gospel," which motivated Disciple pioneers, did not bring a perfect church— a field free of tares. The "restoration" came to include many of the evils of the ancient Corinthian church.

UPROOTING FOREDOOMED TO FAILURE

From all of this we should conclude, with the insight of Jesus' parable, that it is futile and it may even be disastrous to try to achieve a pure church in which there are no sinners.

The rooting up of the tares or the building of fences against such noxious weeds is foredoomed to failure.

The uprooting of the tares is never accomplished without the uprooting of wheat. In their growing stages wheat and tares so closely resemble each other that they cannot be distinguished from each other. Thus it came about that Jerusalem stoned the prophets and killed those whom God sent to her, as Jesus charged. Thus it came about that Jesus himself was crucified outside a city wall; and that prophets are honored more often when they are in their tombs than when they are on their feet. A living prophet is hard to distinguish from a criminal, and is often treated as such. In this there is no reason to suppose that the twentieth century is different from all the foregoing centuries. Some of our contemporaries who are most hated now will turn out, when the verdict of the centuries is in, to have been our choicest and farthest-seeing spirits. Such is the peril of trying to uproot the tares—it results in the uprooting of the choicest wheat.

But there are other reasons why the attempt to eradicate error from the church is misguided. For one thing, the church by its very nature gathers in all kinds and conditions of men, in all stages of moral and spiritual growth. This truth is fully illuminated by the companion parable of the Dragnet (Matt. 13:47-50). The church is like that; it gathers in good and bad together. It is not the assignment of men, but of God and his angels at the judgment, to make the separation; to decide who has lived a good life and who has not. If the church were intended to be a realm of moral and spiritual perfection, this would not be the case. But if it is to be a realm of redemption it must include slaves who are learning how to put off their chains. If it is to be a realm of education it must take in the

119

ignorant and unlettered, that they may be led into all truth. If it is to heal diseases it must take in the sick; else there is little use for the Great Physician. The church is not utopia; it is a battleground where ancient armies of God and Satan clash by night and where the prize is man's immortal soul. So long as the invitation of the church says, "Whosoever will may come," there will be evil and error in the church. The tares will grow amidst the wheat until the harvest.

Another reason why the attempt to eradicate false prophecy from the church is futile or even pernicious is found in the identity of the false prophet. Who is he? Men are fond of pretending that he is something or somebody outside us—evil men, evil systems. But the tares, in the last analysis, are not other churches or other denominations; they are not even other people. They are immaturities and impurities in our own attitudes. The Christian soldier battles "not against human foes, but against cosmic powers . . . against the superhuman forces of evil" in the dark abyss of our egocentric anxieties and hostilities, and against the evil momentum of ancient wrong hallowed by custom and perpetuated by cowardice.

In *The Enemy Below,* a movie directed by the late Dick Powell, actor Robert Mitchum cast as the commander of a destroyer was talking with a fellow officer about the impending end of World War II. "When the war is over" he said, "our troubles will not be ended. Evil is a snake. Cut off its head, and another head grows back; because it is not in other people. It's in us; and we can't kill it."

The wheat and the tares grow together. This says something to our dream of achieving a pure religion refined of human error. The accomplishments of science may have led us to hope for this. Science has left much of its chambered past behind on the shore of life's unresting sea. Alchemy has become chemistry. Astrology has grown into astronomy. And medicine with its purges, its bleeding bowls, and its leeches has become modern, scientific medicine. May we not expect as much of religion?

One clue to an answer is to ask a few questions about the personal and social life of the scientist. Is he unfailingly a faithful husband and a wise father? Is he always a benevolent, far-seeing citizen, who handles his money generously and charitably for the general welfare? Is he free of racial prejudice? Or is he, like other people, plagued by his own personal immaturities—driven by wild sexual appetites, subject to anger and to greed like other men, a victim of divorce and of guarding his own vested interest against the needs of the disenfranchised? We are well aware of the fact that there are vast areas of life that the scientist's science does not touch and that in these areas the problems of maturity are much the same for him as for all the rest of us. He may be as baffled as we are by a teen-age son or daughter, as uncertain as we are when entering a voting booth. For though he is a scientist, he is a man, and he has no choice but to struggle with these personal and social issues. He is a person and he cannot neglect the issues of being a person.

Now the sphere of religion is the sphere of the personal. By *personal* I do not mean *private*. The personal question is the question of our *identity* and of our *relationships*. Who are we? How are we related—to our own self-awareness and self-acceptance, to our kith and kin, to our fellow-citizens and neighbors, and to the ultimate issue of *being* in the living universe? In the sphere of the personal, life can be mature or immature; it can be encounter or escape; it can grow into

121

life, or under many disguises it may dash headlong into death. The ancient text of religion, attributed to Moses, is this: "I have set before you life and death, blessing and curse; therefore choose life, that you and your descendants may live" (Deut. 30:19).

In actual practice, of course, we are neither wholly mature nor wholly immature. The best that we can hope for is that we are maturing. We are neither wholly courageous in facing life's issues, nor are we wholly cowards. The best that we can hope for is that we may grow to be less and less refugees from history and more and more actors in its drama.

The thing that concerns us is this mixture of the immature with the mature. We find it in religion, and we will continue to find it there. The human race can leave alchemy, astrology, and bad medicine behind, but it is doubtful if the race can leave bad religion behind—not completely. We are too close to our elemental needs to rationalize our unrecognized rebellion against God under the conscious pretense of serving him. The pain of seeing the full blaze of truth is blinding to eyes accustomed to twilight and dark. So while there will be a divine call for the prophets and seers, there will also be a popular demand for the false prophet, for the non-seer who will "speak to us smooth things." Because religion is the realm of the personal and of our ultimate concern, we seek within it escape and self-salvation. We look there to find support for our childishness, guarantees of our false securities, insulation against the high voltage of the living God.

Religion is the realm of ultimate concern, and, therefore, of confrontation with ultimate good and ultimate evil. Among the documents drawn upon by some writers of the Old Testament was a lost book which they named *The Book of the Wars of the*

Lord (Num. 21:14). That is a good name for the whole Bible. It is the Book of the Wars of God. But who is God's adversary? There are some who would make it man himself. But Christ has shown us that God is for us, not against us. The adversary is the demonic in the depths of our own being and in the inherited structures of social wrong plus whatever metaphysical rootage the demonic may have. To this demonic force, or these demonic forces, tradition does not hesitate to assign the name Satan. The battleground between God and Satan is the human soul—not the isolated human soul—but the soul as person in identity and in relationship. The principal place where this battle is joined is the church. Jesus rebuked the young man who addressed him as "Good Teacher." No one is good save God. Perhaps it is time for him to rebuke us for calling the church good. No church is good; only God is good; but in the church, the battle is joined between the darkness and the light.

The tares are Satan's sowing; they are planted, not in their own plot, but in the midst of the wheat. Those who are entrusted with the cultivation of God's acre have an almost uncontrollable urge to rush into the field and begin uprooting the tares. But this is both futile and evil.

JUDGE NOT BEFORE THE TIME

We must let the wheat and the tares grow together until the harvest. Then they will be separated. The wheat will then be stored in the granary; the tares will be burned in fire.

Jesus here speaks of the judgment. Not the judgment of men but the judgment of God. Because human judgment is fallible and self-righteous, Jesus warned, "Judge not, that you be not judged. For with the judgment you pronounce you will be judged, and the measure you give will be the measure you get" (Matt. 7:1-2). Paul, in much the same vein, said, "Beloved, never avenge yourselves, but leave it to the wrath of God; for it is written, 'Vengeance is mine, I will repay, says the Lord!'" (Rom. 12:19).

In the present study we have seen sound reasons for the warning. For, unless we leave the judgment to God, we will get caught in the logic of inquisition or of suicide.

But what does this leave us? Are we condemned to fold our hands and do nothing? Does this mean that we are to resign ourselves to evil? Does it require us to wait in patience until death and the great assize? If we are to take it seriously, this teaching certainly does mean an end to bloody crusades and inquisitions. But it does not mean quiescence and passivity.

First we had better relocate the judgment, not at the end of chronological time—*chronos*—but at the apex of time as opportunity—*kairos*. The judgment of God is God's ultimate measure being placed against our lives. It is the Almighty's plumb line held to the leaning wall of our endeavor. It is final not in the sense of being at the *end* of time but in the sense of being *over* time, in the sense of being ultimate and without appeal. Bastard wheat may look so much like wheat that no human eye can detect the difference, but God knows the difference. Man looks on the outward appearance, but God looks upon the heart.

Second, we had better see what this means about the quality of our meeting when we gather in the house of God. It means that we gather there not to become the vengeance of God against the unrighteous—ourselves being the righteous. It means that we gather there in repentance, under the judgment and the grace of God. It means further that our relationships

124

with our fellows are such as will enable them to meet with us in confession and repentance. We may warn them, with what skill we possess, when we see them in need of warning, but we do not threaten them; we may warn them but we do not punish them. If we are called upon to speak the surgical truth, we speak it not in anger but in love.

Third, we had better recognize that this means opening up to the searching eye of God not only our sins but also our ideals. This is because of the nature of evil; it does not tempt us until it disguises itself. It masquerades as goodness. We may be very sure of this: Somewhere among our ideals we are holding to something as good which is hateful to God. Only as his love casts out our fear; only as we stop defending ourselves, rationalizing and projecting to appear righteous in our own eyes; only as we come before God open and undefended will we be able to recognize some of these hidden sins.

There is a memorable passage in Paul's correspondence with the Corinthians which we will do well to ponder:

This is how one should regard us, as servants of Christ and stewards of the mysteries of God. Moreover it is required of stewards that they be found trustworthy. But with me it is a very small thing that I should be judged by you or by any human court. I do not even judge myself. I am not aware of anything against myself, but I am not thereby acquitted. It is the Lord who judges me. Therefore do not pronounce judgment before the time, before the Lord comes, who will bring to light the things now hidden in darkness and will disclose the purposes of the heart. Then every man will receive his commendation from God (I Cor. 4:1-5).

Where is the false prophet? Who is a false prophet? He is here, in our midst, in you and in me. There are times when we are true and times when we are false. It may be well for us to remember that Jesus met with this kind of fraudulence among the twelve disciples. A. T. Cadoux has observed:

We probably do not appreciate the strain which events put upon the loyalty of the twelve: the wonder is not that Judas fell away, but that others did not. Jesus seems to have recognized that Peter, James and John were reliable, but unless in some of the rest there was something like that which moved Judas, what was the point of saying, "One of you shall betray me?" [4]

In the light of this it is no less appropriate for us than for them to ask, "Lord, is it I?"

We may not be Judas in the end, but certainly we have had our moments. The best that we can hope for under the eye of one who knows fraud when he sees it, is that we shall be made aware of our own fraudulence, in time to repent.

[4] A. T. Cadoux, *The Parables of Jesus* (London: James Clarke & Co., 1930), p. 159.

What Then Shall We Do?

Repent. And bring forth fruits worthy of repentance.

To say this to ministers of the gospel may seem to be an effrontery. It is an indispensable part of the minister's message *to others*. Without it there can be no forgiveness of sins, no acquittal before the bar of God's judgment, no self-acceptance, no restoration of broken human relationships, no knowledge of God's grace, no power of the Holy Spirit. Perhaps ministers assume that they have repented—that their priestly function in the penitence of others becomes their own penitence. It is a false assumption. For ministers, in addition to the ordinary failings of other men, are tempted by special sins that arise from their nearness to the altar. And unless they live penitently, they will live arrogantly or despairingly.

Again, ministers tend to coast on past acts of contrition. Perhaps there was a day, a memorable day, when they crossed the great divide between life and death by costly turning from self to God. The radiance of that hour was so great that it cast its light far down the years. But it is a light that grows dimmer with each passing month of life's outward voyage. For repentance is not only a single deed, done once for all time, like a wedding ceremony; it also has to be continued daily, like a marriage, in renewing words and deeds. To live without fresh repentance is to live from melting resources.

Repentance is mighty. It must not be confused with remorse. Or vain regret. Or good resolutions. Or self-pity. The thing that passes for repentance is often a feeble counterfeit. It is not the lifting of the shoulders in a self-excusing shrug. It is the lifting of the hands to God in genuine contrition.

Genuine repentance is at once the *least we can do* and the *most we can do*. It is the least of human actions because it has so little to do with *activities*. It deals not with what we do so much as with who we are—the kind of persons we acknowledge ourselves to be when we stand in the full light of God's truth. This calls for a kind of courage far greater than that summoned up for any action, even heroic action. It calls for the courage to be humiliated, stripped of every self-justification whatsoever. It calls for the courage to come before the living God and *die*. As such, repentance is a deed which has very little resemblance to "doing something." It is the deed of relationship which sets us where we belong in our very beings as dependent creatures, offspring of the Eternal, yet bent upon having our own way and being our own gods. Repentance is the least of human deeds and, therefore, the mightiest of deeds. People say they would rather die than repent—they find it that difficult; and for want of repentance millions are dying every day.

Repentance is also the *most we can do*. It is that because it is the profoundest means by which we can stop acting from our own meager resources as our own architects and saviors and begin to let God act out of his bounty. Through repentance and repentance alone the old man may die so that the new man may be born. It is God who gives this second birth. The life of the spirit that springs from this rebirth is a gift, not a human achievement, just as our biological birth and life are God's gifts to us. Therefore, repentance, the least of deeds and the hardest of all human actions, is the greatest of deeds. It opens the door for God's mighty act of deliverance. In terms of personhood, in terms of authenticity, it is the most important thing we can do.

The genuine spokesman of God lives daily under repentance.

AUTHENTICITY NOT CONTRIVED

The necessity for genuine, costly repentance becomes still clearer when the matter is viewed in another light. The sign of authenticity is not the clenched fist. It is the open hand. Though the Word of God may be received by those who are open to it, it may not be coerced by those who aspire to become its masters. The role of the true prophet is that of *servant of the Word*. When the Word is God's, no other role is possible. In a fine essay on *preaching*, Walter Luthi has rightly said, "True authority is an act of grace. . . . No man has the power to summon the presence of the Word of God. Here the preacher is distinguished from the sorcerer who thinks that he can compel God by chanting formulas." [1] The preacher is not a

[1] Walter Luthi and Eduard Thurneysen, *Preaching, Confession, the Lord's Supper.* (Richmond: John Knox Press, 1960), p. 13.

sorcerer but a servant, because true authority is an act of grace. And grace is conferred only upon the contrite.

In a careful essay in German, Eva Osswald concludes that there are no sure, external criteria that can be set up to determine when a prophet is really transparent to the divine. Authenticity cannot be packaged and labeled. Each spokesman and each oracle must be judged by God himself in relation to the prophet's own place and appointed hour. In general, however, the message of the prophet is to be tested by its ethical consistency. Moreover, it is closest to truth when it speaks judgment; closest to error when it promises painless salvation.[2] The prophet, then, is above all a voice of warning to a world bent on destruction. That is to say, he comes like John the Baptist at the Jordan and like Jesus entering Galilee, calling, "Repent, for the kingdom of heaven is at hand." Since true prophecy, fundamentally, is a call for repentance, shall the prophet himself be unrepentant?

NO GENERAL REPENTANCE

This brings us to a more specific word on repentance itself, especially that repentance appropriate to a herald of the Word. To begin with, it is necessary to remember that no one can repent for another. Like dying, one must do it for oneself. The minister who feels that he has no need of repentance is in need of it most of all.

In the next place, to be real, repentance must be specific. There is no such thing as repentance in general. Sin—even the sin of false prophecy—is a state of disorientation or es-

---

[2] Eva Osswald, *Falsche Prophetie im Alten Testament* (Tubingen: B. Mohn, 1962).

trangement, but it has specific manifestations. To be sure, a man must do more than repent of isolated sins. He must repent of sin itself—that is to say, of self-elevation, of inordinate desire, and of unbelief and idolatry—but he must come to recognize the many subtle ways in which sin becomes incarnate in himself, through actual attitudes, words, and deeds which he can date as to time and locate as to place.

It is for this reason that no one may take lightly, and as of no significance to himself, the marks of the false prophet disclosed by the present study. What minister is entirely free of the temptations of conspicuous righteousness, "to be seen of men"; or of being well-liked? Is there anyone standing behind a pulpit who has not given silent consent to great social wrongs in order to remain in good standing with members of his church who are too deeply mired in those wrongs? Who has not tasted the heady intoxication of power that leadership brings, and who does not cling to and desire that power for himself? What man is free of petty annoyance and not-so-petty resentments against "obstreperous" parishioners? The minister who confessed to naming his golf balls after his most cantankerous elders and deacons needs a kind of recreation that cannot be provided at the country club.

Further specifics pile up, like closely packed cars in a traffic jam. It is easy to confuse "the American Way of Life" with Christianity, to mistake Uncle Sam for Jesus Christ. Patriotism and religion mix and mingle in the affection of ministers just as they do in other people. The tendencies toward comfort and self-indulgence which make Americans "soft" in this seventh decade of the twentieth century incline clergymen as well as others toward easy living. It is not difficult to be concerned primarily about salary, parsonage, pension, and car allowance; and only secondarily about gospel, persons, and ministerial mission. To be concerned about one's success as the executive of a thriving organization is easier than to be concerned about wayward prodigals and rebellious elder brothers in the congregation. Many ministers tend to feel that they should be given special credit or some extra merit simply because they are ministers: rebates in department stores, discounts in garages, and extra "stars in their crown" at the final judgment. It is difficult not to believe that we always live up to our own preaching. To have said it so smoothly slips over into supposing that we have practiced it.

Need we go further? Are there no sermons that have been slighted in preparation—fitted out with predigested ideas lifted from other thinkers? Do we always resist the temptation to justify and defend ourselves and to leave vengeance to God? Have we never judged another minister or a layman harshly?

The list could be extended, but let it suffice as it stands. If the Apostle Paul could write, "I pommel my body and subdue it, lest after preaching to others I myself should be disqualified" (I Cor. 9:27), surely the most of us dare not rest lightly upon our ministerial laurels. Rather, like Paul, it is altogether fitting that we stand among our people as God's heralds "in weakness and in much fear and trembling" (I Cor. 2:3). The minister, in order to grow progressively away from the outward show toward the inner reality of his office, needs to live habitually under repentance.

FRUITS WORTHY OF REPENTANCE

Repentance is turning—but it is more than turning away from. It is turning toward. I like to think that it includes not only contrition, confession, and restitution—which it most certainly does—but also *captivation*. It is only as a man comes under the power of ultimate concern and ultimate commitment—when he is drawn, not driven—that his turning becomes a genuine turning to God. Then it is not he who chooses God, but God who chooses him. His insufficient power is filled up by sufficing grace. God has made him captive—and made him free.

Captivation has its disciplines, not the duty-drugged disciplines of self-salvation and killing legalism, but the disciplines of a great affection. Disciplines like those of a teenager captivated by electronics. Under his own power he learns more about radio, television, and space exploration than a dozen renowned physicists could drive into his head in years of coercive instruction. Disciplines like those of the pianist who practices eight hours daily—drawn by his love of music, not driven by any taskmaster.

WITHDRAWAL AND RETURN

We have said that the false prophet is captured by culture and trapped in the temple. What is the discipline of a higher captivation in these realms? Following Arnold Toynbee, I want to call it the discipline of withdrawal and return.

Every preacher of the Word has a deep need to "get away from it all" at fairly regular and frequent intervals. This is a need for something considerably more important than a vacation. It is the need to escape the rut, to get a new perspective upon oneself and one's job; the need to gain new insights and gather new resources. It is an important element in the role we must all play as strangers and pilgrims, and as Christ's ambassadors. The trouble with most of us most of the time is that we are bound in the graveclothes of habit and custom, boxed in by momentary goals and trivial views, and buried six feet under a weight of demands and duties. We do "let the world around us squeeze us into its own mold, and we do not let God remold our minds from within" (paraphrase of Rom. 12:2, Phillips). No wonder we fail to "prove that the plan of God for us is good, or that it meets all his demands and moves us toward the goal of true maturity"!

What we are dealing with here is the rhythm of creativity. Arnold Toynbee devoted a considerable section of his book *The Study of History* to it under the title "Withdrawal and Return." "The withdrawal," Toynbee wrote, "makes it possible for the personality to realize powers within himself which might have remained dormant if he had not been released for the time being from his social toils and trammels. Such a withdrawal may be a voluntary action on his part or it may be forced upon him by circumstances." Thus, to use an illustration that occurs to me, Viktor Frankl's enforced withdrawal from Vienna into the Auschwitz death camp under the Nazis resulted in his creation of a whole new branch of psychotherapy called "logotherapy," and in the writing of his powerful book, *From Death-Camp to Existentialism*. From withdrawal, be it voluntary or enforced, transfiguration may result.

Such withdrawal is creative, however, only if it is intimately wedded to return. Toynbee continued,

A transfiguration in solitude can have no purpose, and perhaps even no meaning, except as a prelude to the return of the transfigured personality into the social milieu out of which he had originally come: a native environment from which the human social animal cannot permanently estrange himself without repudiating his humanity and becoming, in Aristotle's phrase, "either a beast or a god." The return is the essence of the whole movement as well as its final cause. [3]

Having stated this principle of creativity through withdrawal and return, Toynbee illustrated it at great length from the biographies of famous men and from the histories of creative minorities. It was, for instance, the pattern of the Exodus: Moses withdrew from urban Egypt to the contemplation of the Midianite desert and the life of a shepherd. He returned to lead his people out of bondage. Paul withdrew from Damascus to the Arabian desert, and after three years returned to become the flaming evangel to the Gentiles. Jesus withdrew from the crowds at the Jordan to the barren heights of the Judean wilderness to linger in contemplation forty days and nights. He returned to society heralding the coming of God's kingdom. This pattern of withdrawal and return was, in fact, a constant rhythm in the life of the Master. It was apparently his daily practice to withdraw from the demanding crowds and even from his own disciples into a place apart where he could be alone with his Father. The transfiguration has to be understood in such a light, as do his walking tour of the borders of Tyre and Sidon, the lingering at Caesarea Philippi, the Last Supper, and the lonely vigil in Gethsemane.

If we are to be creative spokesmen for such a Master, there is no reason to suppose that we can escape the necessity of submitting to this pulsebeat of eternity. If we withdraw it must be for renewal and transfiguration. We must return with new vigor and new purpose in order to serve.

[3] Arnold J. Toynbee, *The Study of History*. Abridged by D. C. Somervell (New York: Oxford University Press, 1947), p. 217.

We may do this not in one but in many ways. We must withdraw from the noisy world of television and from the pulpy jungle of the newspaper. That is to say, we must withdraw from instant news on the hour and the half hour to voices that speak for the years and centuries. If all we breathe is the dust kicked up by "Wagon Train," we will choke to death.

One path that leads out of this choking dust is the minister's annual vacation—or it may be such a path. This may even include a trip abroad. However, it is harder to get out of America than we may think. The ship that takes you across the ocean may be a floating American island. The world capitals in which you stop will have their American quarters. With only a little trying, you can eat American food, read American newspapers, listen to American radio and drink Coca-Cola clear around the world. And you can return to America from a complete circuit of the globe without ever having been out of the country.

To escape from America is difficult. To escape from Western civilization is even more difficult. We cannot do it by going to Europe or South America. Only in the Near East and the Far East is there the slightest possibility that we may do it, even to a small degree. But, it is clear, if we can *really* withdraw from America and from Western civilization for a time, and if we do not insist upon packing America and Western civilization in our luggage and carrying them with us everywhere, we may glimpse a new vision and return with a new sense of mission.

Another path that leads us into the hills of solitude and transfiguration is that of books. Still another is the path of prayer. And yet another is that of conferences and retreats. But the road that leads to the highland of the Bible is always at hand. It is only through living on this tableland day by day that we have any real chance of becoming pilgrims and sojourners, let alone ambassadors. The German poet Heinrich Heine, noting that the Jews for centuries were deprived of a homeland, explained the continuing history of the Jewish people when he said that in the Bible they had a "portable fatherland." This is *our* Father's land, too, our own, our native land as Christian heralds. Only to the extent that we live in this fatherland is there any real hope of living in creative tension with our culture and its institutions in this twentieth century.

THE DISCIPLINE OF THE WORLD

The real captivation of the Christian herald requires something more. It demands a return, but something more than a return to the study and the sanctuary. It requires a return to the common life in the midst of the people.

Too often our involvement with people is restricted to meetings with them in "church work," when, in the nature of the case, they are abstracted from their daily immersion in domestic and vocational entanglements. We need to know our people individually, by name, but also in terms of their daily struggles. This will require a vast amount of pastoral labor.

It will also require community service. In a lively autobiographical volume, *I Would Do It Again,* the late F. E. Davison told the story of his life as a Christian minister. One of the things he would do again appears as a chapter heading, "I Would Serve My Community." In this connection he wrote about courts, police, and social agencies:

When I had been in [a new] . . . pastorate for about a year I decided that I should have more specific information about certain agencies and resources of the community in which I lived. So I set aside one week to study the courts, another for the social agencies, and still others for the police department, the labor unions, and the motion picture houses. In advance I wrote letters to those in charge and asked for the privilege of visiting their agencies. I received cordial cooperation in every case. As a means of making myself give close attention to what I saw, I announced to my men's Forum Club that I would bring them a series of messages on "Out of the Week"—"Out of the Week with the Labor Union," "the Police Department," etc. These messages were carefully prepared, and the newspapers gave fine coverage of what was said.

The judges not only permitted me to sit in their courtrooms but gladly gave me time for interviews concerning their work and decisions. During a similar project in a Chicago court, I once sat beside the judge and heard him hand down a number of decisions. In one case, when the evidence was all in, the judge turned to me and said in an undertone, "Well, Mr. Preacher, you decide this one, and I will follow your suggestion. . . ."

My visits to the various social agencies were not only a refresher course in sociology but gave me a better idea of where to refer many of the cases that come under my observation and counsel. One cannot possibly visit the crippled children's clinic, the orphans' home, and the out-patient section of the hospital without experiencing a new desire to help meet the social needs of the community. No minister can be worthy of his title unless he is willing to throw a large part of his life into meeting those needs.

During the week spent with the police, I was introduced to the detective department, the record department, the lie detector . . . and the "drunkometer." Two nights I spent cruising about the city in squad cars. Through conversation with the patroling officers, I discovered a side of my city's life which I had hardly known existed.[4]

[4] F. E. Davison, *I Would Do It Again* (St. Louis: The Bethany Press, 1948), pp. 116-17.

No one who knew "Davy," the author of the above account, ever accused him of being trapped in the temple. He was too firmly captivated by his people, too alert to the daily pressures bearing upon them, ever to let himself become imprisoned within the confining walls of the religious institution.

REMOVING THE MASK

It now remains only to lay down a few constructive proposals about the unmasking of the ministerial Pharisee.

Why does anyone hide behind a mask? Because he is afraid. A man puts forward a mask because he is afraid that his natural face is too uncomely to be accepted. In a word, he does not really accept himself. He is still suing for God's acceptance; and with people he lives in a state of siege. This condition may be so deep and so habitual that he is not really aware of it. It is a preconception rather than a conception, an attitude rather than an awareness. To be is to be in relationship. This man, in his relationships, is living in a state of distortion or separation from himself, from his God, and from his fellows. He is, however, trying to work his way out of this impasse into the favor of man and God, and into his own self-respect. This is another way of saying that he is living under law, not under grace. It is curious, but true, that a man may live under law although he *believes* in grace, and even though he *preaches* grace.

Just as a man cannot see his own face by direct vision, but must look in a mirror, so a man cannot by introspection see himself. To serve as mirror he needs the face of a candid and concerned companion. Other people read us far better than we like to acknowledge. When they read us and at the same time cast us aside or hold us at arm's length, there is nothing for us to do but resist their judgment and fight for our lives. But when, among those that read us, there are those who speak the truth *in love,* accepting us although we are unacceptable, it is no longer necessary to fight back or to pretend to ourselves that we are other than we are. In the face of a candid and concerned companion we can come to see ourselves as we are; but, more than that, we can break through into God's grace. The church makes itself present to us in the presence of our brother. The priesthood of believers becomes a reality in place of a dogma, for where two or three are gathered in this spirit, Another is there in transforming power.

Since what I have just written is attested by nearly twenty years of experience in the teaching of seminarians to preach, it may not be amiss here to go a little more deeply into detail.

As long as a man is immersed in "the neurotic culture of our time" with its bitter competitiveness, he is in no condition to seek the truth or to accept it when it is shown to him. For this reason, in preaching classes we do not raise the question, "What is this man saying emotionally?" until the class has been welded into a community of mutual concern, and most of the defensiveness has been dissolved. Then we ask each member of the class to answer three questions about each man as he appears in the pulpit: "How does he feel about himself as a person? What feelings does he project toward us? What emotional response does he 'kick up' in us?" These questions get at the realm of interpersonal relations, which is the realm of our being as persons. It is amazing how perceptive a group can be in such a setting.

For the preacher, the experience of being faced with the truth about himself is traumatic. What he has been unable even to see, much less to accept, is suddenly thrust upon him. It is thrust upon him in such a setting that he cannot write it off as the libel of an enemy or the misunderstanding of a stranger. He may be able to accept it—or he may learn to accept it in time—because it is offered to him by friends who accept him already, just as he is and for himself alone. Without their concern he could not have listened to their candor. Both candor and concern are necessary; but the concern must come first and it must be the greater of the two.

What is begun in such a fellowship of truth and love can be carried forward in quiet meetings with a single counselor. These meetings may extend, once a week, over a period of many weeks or months until a man has come to know "in his bones" the reality and power of the paradox of God's grace—"accepted though unacceptable." It can happen. I have seen it happen many times. A man need not labor under law; he can live under grace—but he cannot do it alone.[5]

CONCLUSION

This has not been a comforting book, nor is it meant to be. We are living through a time in which the church is coming under fresh bombardment. Its critics are many; not the least prominent among these critics are members of the clergy. But clergy and church go together. It may be said, in general, that no church may be expected to go where its clergy does not lead. If the contemporary church suffers from coldness, con-

[5] Those wishing further light on this topic are referred to Chapter 7, "What Are You Saying Emotionally," in the book, by Dwight E. Stevenson and Charles F. Diehl, *Reaching People from the Pulpit* (New York: Harper & Row, 1958).

fusion, and conformity, it may not be amiss to examine the temperature of the church in the neighborhood of the pulpit. Unless there is authenticity there—or, at the very least, the agonizing struggle for authenticity—how can we expect to find it elsewhere?